GRACE

On the Journey to God

GRACE

On the Journey to God

MICHAEL CASEY, OCSO

PARACLETE PRESS
BREWSTER, MASSACHUSETTS

2020 Third printing
2019 Second printing
2018 First printing

Grace: On the Journey to God

Copyright © 2018 by Michael Casey

ISBN 978-1-64060-064-5

Library of Congress Cataloging-in-Publication Data

Names: Casey, Michael, 1942- author.
Title: Grace : on the journey to God / Michael Casey, OCSO.
Description: Brewster, MA : Paraclete Press, Inc., 2018. |
Includes bibliographical references.
Identifiers: LCCN 2017059864 | ISBN 9781640600645 (trade paper)
Subjects: LCSH: Grace (Theology) | Benedictines--Spiritual life. | Spiritual
life--Catholic Church. | Christian life--Catholic authors. | Spirituality--
Catholic Church.
Classification: LCC BT761.3 .C37 2018 | DDC 234--dc23
LC record available at https://lccn.loc.gov/2017059864

10 9 8 7 6 5 4 3

Published by Paraclete Press
Brewster, Massachusetts
www.paracletepress.com

Printed in the United States of America

Contents

Introduction

The title of this book is very general: *Grace: On the Journey to God*. It is made up of a series of reflections on what we are likely to experience when we begin to give ourselves conscientiously to the spiritual journey. The closer we come to the end of this journey we are more probably inclined to agree with Georges Bernanos's character at the end of *The Diary of a Country Priest* that grace is everywhere.[1] The benevolence of God expresses itself in so many different ways as our journey unfolds. Gradually we come to realize that everything that happens in our life is somehow the gift of our loving Father. Occasionally this is apparent at the time; most often it happens in retrospect when the elements of wisdom are beginning to find a place in our hearts. This is why I have included the word *grace* in the titles of all the chapters in this book.

My aim is to be mainly descriptive, to talk about experiences we may have on our spiritual journey, and to throw in some historical or theological parallels in the hope that you, the reader, may recognize yourself in what I say and take the giant step of concluding that perhaps you are normal after all. I cannot repeat too often: what you hear within your own spirit is more significant than what I say. My aim is to help you to listen to the voice of God in your heart. So, this book attempts to be an exercise in increasing our levels of spiritual literacy—our capacity to read what is happening in our spiritual life, what the Holy Spirit is accomplishing in our souls at this time. Sometimes what we feel surpasses our powers to describe it, and this is where we are obliged to extend the scope of our spiritual vocabulary, to find words that can adumbrate what we are experiencing. It is also an invitation to look back on past years and to wonder at what God has done in our lives. This is the frequent admonition of the book of Deuteronomy: Remember! Although we have to keep our eyes on the goal and look ahead to the future, we also have to remain in contact with the pattern of God's action in the past. This is the work that leads to wisdom—as it were to extract all the juice from what our years of discipleship have taught us.

In this matter of spiritual literacy, it is always useful to operate within a tradition. This is why, over the past century, fervent Catholics have often attached themselves to one or other tradition or movement within the Church, supplementing what they received from their home parish with a formation and support that seemed to accord with their own spiritual aspirations.[2] You will not fail to notice how heavily I am reliant on the great writers of the Benedictine and Cistercian tradition, especially Aelred of Rievaulx and Bernard of Clairvaux. The overt references are only the part of the iceberg visible above the surface. There is much more dependence on these sources that is underneath and is invisible even to myself. This ancient and well-tried tradition may not be very familiar to you, but you will certainly discover points of contact with your own approach. There is some advantage in looking at familiar matters from a different perspective, and it is my hope that the tradition that has nurtured me these many years may be helpful to you, the reader, in your own particular situation.

This book came to birth as a series of retreat conferences given to religious communities in different countries, and some of my examples and applications are drawn from life in a monastic community. Given my own background and experience, that is probably inevitable. It is my hope, however, that the themes covered are sufficiently general to enable those in other walks of life to find in them echoes of their own experience.

The specific slant that I want to give to this book is to group themes around the word *grace*. We know that there is always a tendency to the ancient heresy of Pelagianism wherever people are a little bit more fervent; the temptation is to put too much emphasis on what they do—sometimes with much effort—and not enough on the invisible action of God's grace. Even poor John Cassian (360–435) was accused of being a Semi-Pelagian because his spirituality was not on the same page as that of Augustine, his more famous contemporary (354–430). So, the point that I want to emphasize is that the most important happenings on our spiritual journey are not the result of our own actions but are gifts of God, given directly or indirectly, including what may seem, at first, to be accidents, tragedies, or disasters. When we fail to detect their source we often misjudge how to respond to them. We have to restate the principle that is surely well-known to us all that what God does to us or for us is far more beautiful and effective than anything we can do to ourselves or for ourselves.

I have included a prayer at the end of each chapter in the hope that the reader may take the opportunity to stop reading and thinking and move into a different space, perhaps to take a few moments for prayerful reflection. I expect that not everything I say will be self-evident and at least some of it may seem counter-intuitive. This is why I recommend that you test what I say against your own experience. I am not infallible; your own experience of the ways of God will be a better guide than anything I write. What I propose is offered merely for your reflection. I am not interested in propounding a systematic theory of the spiritual life; what I offer is an attempt to describe some of the realities we may encounter on our journey, in the hope that you, the reader, may have more success in capturing those fleeting moments when a glimpse of something greater appears and, like the travelers to Emmaus, you find your heart burning as you walk along the road.

Lord God, you are the origin and source of all our good works
And it is by your gift that they attain completion.
Help us all to hear what needs to be heard,
To understand what we hear,
And to do what needs to be done.
We ask this in the name of Jesus, our Lord. Amen!

CHAPTER ONE

The Grace of Discontinuity

E very journey has a beginning. Our earthly career begins when we are conceived and then we are born: both beginnings happen without our active involvement. In contrast, our spiritual journey is said to start with an act of choice on our part—even though, for many of us, our Christian initiation was simply an element in the complex cultural endowment we received in our upbringing. Whether at the dawn of reason, as Saint Thomas Aquinas seemed to think, or later, we had to make a choice to begin to follow a spiritual path—sometimes not just once but through a series of narrowing options. For some of us these free acts of will have eventually led to a deliberately spiritual lifestyle or landed us in some form of intentional or consecrated life or, perhaps, in a monastery.

In the past, the idea of a vocation was more or less restricted to those who embraced the priesthood or the religious life. Recruits often arrived at the decision to enter a seminary or a religious order through a fairly efficient delivery system: Catholic family, Catholic education, positive reinforcement for the idea of vocation, entry into an esteemed religious group. It was all so smooth—even seamless. Those who did not follow this path or those who abandoned it were considered to have "no vocation." To some extent this way of thinking still survives. This is despite the fact that the Second Vatican Council entitled a chapter of *Lumen gentium*, The Universal Vocation to Holiness in the Church.[3] It is true that a vocation is more visible in those who adopt a specifically religious lifestyle, but the fact remains that all Christians have a vocation to holiness that is both a gift and a summons.

Today the old delivery system no longer functions. Instead of a lifelong continuance of the religious conventions of childhood, living a serious Christian life more and more seems like a fairly radical reversal both at the level of values and regarding lifestyle. Making a personal commitment to live a spiritual life demands a positive choice, and usually it depends on some kind of spiritual experience that calls a person to a more fervent practice. Vocation is now more visibly a prime example of what I may call "the grace of discontinuity."

The call to discipleship has always been a summons to make a new beginning. We see this very clearly in Saint Mark's account of the call of the first disciples (Mk. 1:16–20). They *were* fishermen, but Jesus promised, "I will make you to *become* fishers of people."[4] The two verbs are not the same. Those called are to be no longer what they were; they are to become something different. It is the end of one life and the beginning of another. The process by which this new becoming operates is twofold: the fishermen have first "to leave behind" what was previously theirs and "to follow" Jesus into an unknown future. The interior experience of vocation is seen exteriorly as the leaving behind of the past and stepping into a future that cannot be foreseen. To bring about such a dramatic change the experience must have generated a certain energy in the ones called, in order to overcome the inertia that we all experience at the prospect of taking up a challenge.

Between the past that is being left behind and the new future there is a gap that marks the definitive discontinuity between the two phases of life. We could call it a "paradigm shift" to indicate that "an entire constellation of beliefs, values, techniques and so on shared by members of a given community" has been left behind in favor of an alternative worldview.[5] There has been a radical turnaround in our way of looking at the world and in our understanding of our own life. The old order has come to an end. Saint Basil the Great insists that this dying to the old is an essential component in the Christian initiation to a higher life.

> It is necessary, first of all, to make a break with one's past life. This is impossible, according to the Lord's words, unless one is born again. Regeneration, as its name indicates, is a second beginning of life. To begin a second time, it is necessary to finish the first. As in athletics when a double race [there and back] is run, there is a halt or a brief rest between the going and returning so, in changing one's life, it is necessary that there be a death to put an end to the life that was and to make a start with the life that is to follow.[6]

Most of us have a fear of change that is initiated from outside: as the old saying goes, "The devil you know is better than the one you don't know." We are grateful that the world around us is familiar and that whatever happens occurs within a familiar range of possibilities. This allows us to fly on automatic pilot—not having to think too much about the details of daily life. We are secure and comfortable, and that is a good thing, but there is a danger that our feelings of ease may degenerate into complacency, smugness, or even a type of arrogance. We become a little too pleased with ourselves. Habituation dims our powers of perception, and we do not see what could change the way we evaluate our present situation.[7] There is much in life that is uncertain, and it is likely that too much certainty will insulate us from the demands of reality. Experience teaches us that there is a healthy kind of insecurity that helps us to recognize the changeableness of every human situation and admonishes us to remain alert to the indications of change and to be creative in fashioning a response.

Complacency can sometimes bedevil our spiritual life. We
have to be careful that we do not allow the fact that our religious
practice has become more or less routine to lead us into over-
confidence. Unless we have an unusually intense relationship with
a competent spiritual elder or guide, we are likely to overestimate
our progress.[8] "Ignorance more frequently begets confidence than
does knowledge." This reminder comes from Charles Darwin in
his introduction to *The Descent of Man* (1871). His assertion was
confirmed when, in 1999, David Dunning and Justin Kruger of
Cornell University published the results of their experimental
research that found an inverse relationship between competence
and confidence. It seems that those who are incompetent in a
particular area habitually overestimate their ability and their performance, casting the blame on external factors when results fail
to meet their expectations. They do not know enough to recognize
the limits of their knowledge. Those who are more competent blow
their own trumpet less loudly. The more they know, the more they
are aware of what they don't know. A similar effect can be observed
in the spiritual life. Beginners sometimes think they have mastered
the spiritual art in a matter of months or years; veterans are more
likely to be sober in their self-assessment. The more advanced we
are, the less we are satisfied with ourselves and with our progress;
the more conscious we are of a nagging need for some change of
direction.

In addition, we need to remind ourselves of how routines operate
on a moral level. They are very efficient in helping us to do things
without much thought, but they can often imprison us behind a wall
of inattentiveness so that we are not fully present in the actions we
perform. Whether these be sins or good deeds, there is often some
degree of automation involved. Even the practice of the virtues can
make us blind. I can be so committed to my own program of moral
rectitude that I fail even to notice that there are more urgent and
more important situations demanding my attention. Remember

the judgment scene in Matthew's Gospel. Those condemned by the judge asked, puzzled at their rejection, "When did we see you, Lord?" Sins of omission are much more easily overlooked by ourselves than sins of commission. It may happen that I have constructed my own version of spiritual life as it seems right and proper to me, without becoming aware of how rigid and unseeing the end product is. Not only is this the case for hard-liners and strict observers, but the same imperviousness can also be found in those who embrace an easygoing philosophy of minimalism. In this situation, whether we are trapped behind walls of virtue or vice, we are not making any progress. We are walking around in circles. "The one who walks in a circle is moving, but he is not getting anywhere."[9] To continue as we are risks a loss of liveliness in our lives. Routine rules and none dare challenge its authority![10]

In most cases we are happy enough with things as they are. We do not see what we cannot see. We do not know what we do not know. This is why sometimes we need to pray for the grace of self-doubt—which may be described as the Scriptures often say of fear of God, as the beginning of wisdom. Occasionally we ought to interrupt our lifelong paeans of self-congratulation and begin to wonder whether some things could be improved. We need to ask whether we have placed limits in our lives from which we need to break out: limits to our prayer, limits to our *lectio divina*, limits to our participation in family or community life, limits to our compassion, limits to our service, limits to the honor we show to others. If we are to advance on the spiritual path, it is quite likely that we will need the assistance of the grace of discontinuity—the willingness to see the need to move in a new direction and, then, to make a break.

From time to time in our life we will become aware of a call to conversion. Because this is a very familiar term there is the possibility that we all attach our own (often reductive) meaning to it. The New Testament word *metanoia* signals that the basic component of the process is a change at the level of intellect; first of all, it involves seeing things differently. Following Bernard Lonergan we may define conversion as a change in perceptual horizons.[11] When we see things in a different context we begin to change our value system; we realize that a situation is not as we had supposed, and we recognize the need to reevaluate it. Usually when we know more of what is hidden we are more understanding and, as a result, more prudent and more compassionate. In time, the new values will give rise to the corresponding actions, and when the actions are repeated they cohere to form virtues. This is how our lives are gradually renewed.

The point of departure for conversion is not always a life constrained by sinful habits or by unbelief. More often it is an existence characterized by inattention. It happens that, in the providence of God, many people pass through a phase during which, after a few fervent years of spiritual living, their lives seem to lie fallow, in a state of chronic nonurgency or passivity. We let things slip, believing that we need a break, not fully conscious of how long we have let it run. For the time being the spiritual life fades into a state of unproductiveness while we attend to alternative areas of growth. This seems unproductive but, secretly, it can be a state of rest in which, unknowingly, preparations are made for what is to come. Breaking out of this state occurs when a new phase of life signals its arrival with a jolt. Unforeseen events confront us with the prophetic call: "Break up the fallow ground, for it is time to seek the Lord" (Hos. 10:12).

Conversion is a process by which the uncreative sameness of our life is fractured and, in a best-case scenario, we are reoriented toward becoming the kind of person God created us to become. In most serious lives, there are two or three major conversions—each of them accompanied by something akin to crisis. The exact shape these transitions take is unique to ourselves—their elements are drawn from our history and our circumstances—and this is very often a cause of much fretting. We worry especially because we do not conform to the stereotype in our heads and we don't grasp that it is precisely to liberate us from these stereotypes that the process is initiated.

Beyond these major conversions and either deriving from them or leading up to them there are many small course adjustments to be made as we continue our journey. The winds and waves that try to turn us around never abate. No doubt that is why Saint John Cassian in his first *Conference* relays the teaching of Abba Moses on the importance of having an ultimate destination and an immediate goal so that we can take sightings as we progress and avoid wasting our efforts drifting away and then having to come back to our fundamental intent.

Conversion is, therefore, a necessary starting point for the spiritual journey. It is also a necessary device to bring us back on course when we have drifted away. Conversion is not, however, something that we can dutifully manufacture, nor is it something that we can somehow monitor or control. It is a gift, a grace; we cannot bring it about through our own efforts. Because it has its origin outside ourselves, mostly it is unwelcome. We change because, in a sense, there is no alternative. "I can do no other." Often conversion comes after prolonged resistance on our part; the same is true of many vocations.

So, then, how does conversion come to us? Following monastic tradition such as Antony of Egypt and Abba Paphnutius, Saint Aelred of Rievaulx suggests four different channels through which we are inspired to make a change.[12]

1. In some cases there is a moment of acute spiritual intensity unconnected with anything that is happening in the outside world. Those who belong to a faith tradition have a language to describe this experience: "a touch of God," a "stirring," an awakening, an enlightenment, compunction,

vocation. This is experienced as a surge of energy that enables us to take the step so long imagined and so long postponed. "A calling is from God whenever some inspiration has taken possession of our heart and even though we are asleep stirs in us a desire for eternal life and salvation."[13] Compunction is "whatever rouses the soul, by God's grace, from its drowsiness and half-heartedness."[14] The experience is strong enough to make a lifelong impact. Those who lack the vocabulary to describe what they have experienced often spend years trying to puzzle out what it means, going from one ideal to another, never finding one that eases their restless searching. But, for all, life is not the same afterward. For those who give assent to its leading, it results in the radical change of lifestyle that we call "conversion."

2. For others there is an attraction to some good or holy person who seems to embody the future they desire for themselves. This could be a relationship with a living person, or an acquaintance of some saint of another time. How many people have discovered yearnings within themselves through contact with Saint Therese of Lisieux or even Thomas Merton? Such an encounter "edifies"; it makes possible the building of a new life. These models serve as mirrors in which persons can see themselves more clearly: they are means by which they discover their own "deep self." Holy people are for us living testimony that sanctity is not impossible and that when it flowers it has a power of attraction that makes others want to pursue it.

3. The summons to walk a spiritual path can come through the counsel of a wise person. This is especially potent when we feel that we are known and understood by the person giving the advice. When someone whose judgment is trusted deliberately suggests a particular path it is a means by which deep, unformed intimations are given shape and

direction. Often the person in question is unaware of the impact made by their words; what is heard is more potent than what is said. The echo resounding in the heart is the primary agent in a new sense of self that, in turn, grounds the willingness to adopt a new manner of living. When wise persons are in short supply God often makes use of baser means, such as Balaam's donkey (Num. 22:15–35). The means are not important; what matters is the resonance that is stirred up in the soul. Books, liturgical readings, and even homilies can operate in a similar way. I know of someone who was converted by a line in a soap opera, which put into words what he himself had been feeling for a long time and resisting. But hearing the words somehow, by God's grace, gave him the energy to take the step that had been staring him in the face for many years.

4. Finally, God can speak to us through disaster, when the order we have so rigorously imposed on our life is lost and we are left to pick up the pieces. Bereavement, loss of employment, family break-up, serious illness, accidents, even grave sins—these can in a single day destroy the lives we had, and precipitate us into irretrievable crisis. Like Humpty Dumpty, we find everything is broken; it is almost impossible for us to put the pieces back together in the same way they were, and so we have to create a new and, perhaps, higher integration of the elements of our life. In the process, we develop a new self-image and, maybe, a new social identity. Despite being overwhelmed by what seems to be a tragedy, this is, in reality, an opportunity to be liberated from the staleness that was beginning to mark the previous stage of our life and to venture out into unexplored territory.

Sometimes more than one of these influences is operative. The possibility of these forces affecting us in a way that produces results largely depends on our vulnerability; the great obstacle is the condition of spiritual impermeability that the New Testament names "hardness of heart." We will have more to say on this topic at a later stage of our reflections.

There are five somewhat distinct moments that are required for the integrity of conversion or vocation, both of which are really the effects of the gift of faith becoming active in resetting the parameters of our life. The foundation of the process is an *experience* or the accumulation of experiences that brings the person to a tipping point in which a life-changing decision is unavoidable. The second stage is a certain *illumination* of the mind in which the person begins to perceive what had previously been hidden. A door opens in what had hitherto seemed an impenetrable wall and something of the brilliance of eternal light shines upon them, calling out to them as the burning bush did to Moses. Probably Saint Paul's subsequent teaching on the absolute gratuity of grace, independent of any worthiness on the part of the recipient, had its origin in the illumination that flooded his mind at the moment when God elected to intervene in his life. He spent the remainder of his days pondering its significance. The third and crucial step is that, at the level of free will, a person gives *assent* to what has been unveiled. This is not the end of the process. A fourth stage is *practice*, when the moment of assent is repeated and prolonged so that what was experienced begins to influence the mundane choices by which daily life is shaped.[15] Conversion is most often not just a lightning flash; it is more like the slow dawning of light that begins faintly but gradually permeates the whole of existence. The final stage is *stabilization*: when the effect of conversion not only embraces all spheres of activity, but also reaches out in time from the moment of impact until the end of life. Experience leads to illumination, to assent, and to practice and is crowned through perseverance.

The high drama associated with the conversion of Saint Paul should not be taken as normative. For many people conversion is a drawn-out process that may meander through several years and be marked by many false starts and wrong turnings. Augustine took seventeen years before crossing the finishing line—even with the nagging "assistance" of his mother's prayers. Conversion is not only an action by which change is introduced into one's life. It has to become a state in which the change is, as it were, institutionalized in order that it may become a determinant of the decisions made in the years that follow. It is a little like the dominant political party in Mexico: the Institutional Revolutionary Party (*Partido Revolucionario Institucional*). We have to have a permanent revolution, an ongoing conversion. In the language of Latin monasticism, *conversio* is translated into *conversatio* (way of life or lifestyle).

Conversion is more than a change of affiliation, going from one group membership to another. It is not done once and for all and then forgotten. It is more like a lifelong process by which we allow ourselves to be continually challenged to move out from what is familiar and potentially stale into zones of growth that are not necessarily of our own choosing. It introduces a permanent element of discontinuity into our lives that undermines our usual reluctance to do much more than we are doing at present. We have no assurance that what we will encounter on the road ahead will be the same as the situations we have already met and dealt with. The experience of conversion is necessarily fraught with insecurity. It is not a matter of passing from one stable platform to another—it is more like a leap into the unknown. No doubt this is why Kierkegaard spoke of the *leap* of faith.

This is where it becomes important for us to appreciate the role of discontinuity in our life. To some extent, when we become Christian and, even more so, if we happen to enter a monastery, we renounce our citizenship in a rational world. We become citizens of heaven (Phil. 3:20). The normal laws of cause and effect no longer apply. A higher and more mysterious causality operates: the first are made last, the lowly are exalted and the rich are sent empty away. We are in the awkward position of never quite understanding what is happening in and around us. We are drawn into a cloud of unknowing or—to use flashier language—we become involved in a process of self-transcendence that involves our coming forth from our comfort zone and entering on a lifelong journey through unknown regions. The first imperative of such a life is that we yield control. We stop trying to masterplan everything and allow ourselves to go forward guided by the hand of divine providence.

In general, there are three great turning points in the way many experience their spiritual life. We move, as it were, from nowhere to the beginning, from the beginning to the middle, and from the middle to the end. In each case the transition is difficult. In some way, these stages correspond to the three renunciations described by Abba Paphnutius in Cassian's fourth *Conference*. We are led to step aside from the normal life we had followed to take up some form of serious discipleship. Then progressively we have to eliminate the inconsistences of our behavior so that our religion is lived from the heart and not from external restraints. Finally, we have to submit to radical self-transcendence to allow ourselves to be divinized. It may well be that the transitions between these stages correspond to what Saint John of the Cross termed "the obscure night of the senses" and "the obscure night of the spirit," but that is a question beyond my competence and I will leave it for others more qualified to judge.

Our spiritual life begins when our interior faculties are activated by a wake-up call with a persistent summons to pursue a new way of living. We have already spoken a little about this, and it is not difficult to understand. It is often marked by a certain enthusiasm and energy. This enables us to overcome our initial reluctance so that we may begin to perceive some of the benefits of the new path we have chosen. It gives us the courage to take a first step, and then another. But the journey is much longer than that. This first conversion is a beginning, a point of departure. As such it has to be left behind. The future will be qualitatively different; it is not just a question of quantitative growth. Eventually we will discover that unforeseen hazards threaten to block the way ahead.

The second transition is much heavier. It occurs around the midpoint of life, or rather it creates a midpoint in life at whatever age it occurs, so that retrospectively there is a fuzzy demarcation between "before" and "after." In simple terms what happens is this. In the first part of our life we live and make our choices in the context of others' expectations. Whether we seek approval or rebel, we do so with reference to a parental figure of some kind. At first, obviously, it is our parents who, by a system of rewards and punishments (or nonrewards), train us to *do* what is "good" and so, by implication to *be* or to *become* "good," that is, to conform to their expectations. We are considered "good" if we do what they consider good. If we do not act as expected, then we are made to feel that we are deemed "not-good." As we advance in life others take the place of parents: educators, employers, authorities of all kinds, and maybe even friends. Religious authorities can easily slip into this role, identifying virtue with conformity to their pronouncements. We want to be "good" in their eyes. We conform to their expectations. These do not have to be spoken outwardly because, gradually, we internalize their rules so that they become our own. Many of our choices are influenced by this internal parental voice that is sometimes called the superego, and sometimes our image of God gets mixed up in this dynamism. For half our life we try to fulfill the roles others have assigned us.

Our first major crisis occurs when we begin to assert ourselves more fully, to throw off this heteronomy and become our own person. This is more profound than mere adolescent rebellion, which, after all, demands the presence of parents against whom to rebel. We feel the need to stop being "good" and, instead, to be ourselves, without any clear vision of what this involves. We make a preferential option for the unknown. This is not so easy. In the first place it requires us to detach from the substantial affirmation that was linked to our previous persona. We can't be ourselves unless we are somewhat free from the dominance of a need for the approval of those around us. It can happen that our self-approval plummets as well, because we have so fully accepted the roles and rules others assigned us. Because there is often a certain fractiousness in our behavior at this time, we have to deal with others saying, "You used to be so nice!" They do not like us slipping out of the mold they have unconsciously created for us. We are moving toward living more from the "deep self" and less from the "superficial self," and we have to be prepared for the consequences. This is a second conversion; the beginning of a second journey, a journey toward greater authenticity.

The third transition moves us into high spirituality. The state of purity of heart about which the ancient monks sung so rapturously progressively renders the self completely transparent. This means that God is ever more present to the person, since there is no intervening barrier—or to express it another way, the person is more present to, more mindful of God. A collateral effect of this is that the one who is in this state becomes a channel of God's presence and action to others—providing that the others are, at least, somewhat receptive. This is, obviously, the goal of all our spiritual striving, and it usually coincides with many years of fidelity and, as you may guess, advanced years. But progress is not smooth, and there is a great deal of discontinuity between a worthy life and its transcendent culmination.

Much of our wisdom arrives through retrospection. It is only when we have passed through to the other side that we begin to perceive the advantages of the harrowing through which we have passed. This is partly why there is less information available about these final struggles. As a result, the transition is often rendered more difficult by the doubts that are generated by the changes in our experience. For example, we may feel a profound detachment from many of the exercises that previously seemed to bring us closer to God. Our experience of prayer may seem to be progressively emptier of content. The tenets of the Nicene Creed may seem increasingly baffling. Our faith and our devotion seem to have moved in the direction of the apophatic. Most distressing of all our relationship with Jesus Christ seems to have undergone a substantial change. We begin to comprehend what Saint Paul may have meant when he wrote, "If we have known Christ Jesus according to the flesh, we know him thus no longer" (2 Cor. 5:16).

To enter this ultimate state we must also do battle with a number of fierce demons that guard its portals. In the first place, we have to deal with the fact that (usually) we are getting old and that our life is drawing to a close. We are facing the possibility of prolonged debility and the certainty of death. The first response to the realization of this reality is often anger. This is not necessarily expressed by flaming outbursts of recrimination; it is more often a tendency to complain about things that cannot be changed. It may be tinged with an unconscious fear of exclusion or of being left behind. Usually it is a subtle and seething resentment at the inevitable infirmities and indignities of old age, being out of office, the slapdash manner in which things are done nowadays, the complexities of technologies and the obscurities of newspeak.[16] We can be tyrannized by a shadowy nostalgia for the times when things were better. The anger can turn in on ourselves so that we experience a sense of disgust that we are not handling things better. We are angry at ourselves for being angry.[17] Coupled with this anger is an invisible envy directed at those who are now in charge, for their relative youth, their energy, their insouciance, their apparent freedom. There may be a feeling of being pushed to the margins, though it is not unknown that some elders become complicit in their own alienation, cynical at any attempt at inclusion.

Trivialities may disturb our inner peace in a way that disturbs us still more. In such a situation, we need to recognize that unbroken peace is for the next life; for the present we are often called to patient endurance, though this is easier said than done. All this negativity is easily comprehensible, but it takes a mammoth effort to overcome. As Bette Davis famously remarked, "Old age ain't no place for sissies."[18]

That is a commonplace response to aging; those who overcome it attain to a certain mellowness, sweetness of disposition, and wisdom.[19] But there remain other shadows. Not many of our seniors—if they are honest—are ready to join Edith Piaf in singing *Je ne regrette rien* (I regret nothing). They are more likely to latch onto a line from the Canticle of Hezekiah, much quoted in the Latin tradition: *Recogitabo tibi omnes annos meos in amaritudine animae meae* (Isa. 38:15)—"For you I will think over all my years in the bitterness of my soul." This is what might be termed "late-onset compunction." One of the effects of a resurgent self-truthfulness is the recognition of the spottiness of past decades when apparently good actions were soiled by mixed motivations and unworthy agendas often hidden even from ourselves. We may well ask ourselves "Where have all the years of opportunity gone?" Part of the wisdom of seniority is the ability to gauge more objectively the moral quality of past actions and, in so doing, to experience a deep yet subdued sense of regret at what was done, what was left undone, and the imperfect subjective dispositions that underlay the choices made. Such an insight is not based on far-fetched feelings of inferiority or guilt, but on a profound self-knowledge and on ultimate realism in our own regard. The best indicator of wisdom is that we can face such reality with an emergent equanimity.

Perhaps we have witnessed such a state in others or in ourselves. What is happening? It is important to acknowledge that this is not only a normal development but also a desirable one. It means that the impregnability of our self-approval is being eroded.

It may well surprise us to learn that Saint Bernard considered the infusion of bitterness (*immissio amaritudinis*) as one of the major manifestations of divine mercy.[20] "The third manifestation of [God's] mercy was when he visited my heart and brought about a change whereby what was wrongfully sweet became bitter . . . and I began at last to think over in his presence all my years in the bitterness of my soul."[21] We have advanced so far on the way to truth that we become aware of the flaws in the glass.[22] What is past has passed and we are not able to change it, but by becoming aware of it we can change ourselves. Though we may no longer act in the way we used to, a residue of these past actions remains—and it is possible for us to take steps to neutralize it or eliminate it. "This is the summation of spiritual practice: to arrange our present wisely, to think over our past deeds in bitterness of soul, and also to make prudent provision for the future."[23]

In this way, we effect a radical break with our past, we arrive at a deeper conversion that not only concerns conscious activity but also dredges up elements of our past and subjects them to purgation so that they no longer sully our conscience. As the prospect of the radical discontinuity that comes with death begins to seem closer there is a tendency to wash away with tears of compunction whatever defiles the integrity of our past. More and more we become reliant on the mercy of God and dismissive of any claim we might previously have made of merit or worthiness. This new sobriety is a retrospective purification of the soul that works to restore us to baptismal innocence. This is the transformation that brings us to the threshold of heaven. No doubt there is continuity between the way we live and what will happen to us in the next life, but death will mean the discontinuity of all that is familiar and dear, because it is the doorway to a state that will be even more precious. To grasp eternal life with both hands we must let go of what we now have. The disconnect with our own past that we are experiencing is bringing us to a point of freedom and innocence in which our setting forth for our eternal home becomes an increasingly attractive prospect.

O God, restorer and lover of innocence,
Break the chains that hold us captive far from you,
Wake up our hearts to perceive the ways that lead to you
And strengthen us to embrace what we previously feared.
We ask this in the name of Jesus, our Lord.
Amen!

CHAPTER TWO

The Grace of Desire

We were born incomplete, and we remain so all our life. This seems obvious if we think about it for a moment; notwithstanding this fact, many people waste too much energy lamenting the fact that they are not perfect and feel that their lives are far from complete.[24] In some this leads to ill-advised efforts to remedy the defect by compulsive efforts at self-improvement; in others it generates a kind of desperation that causes them to lose heart and to stop trying.[25] The way to reduce the anguish inherent in both these extremes is to adopt a developmental approach to life in general as well as to the spiritual journey. Life has a beginning, a long middle, and an end; we attempt to skip intermediary stages at our peril. Unless we are interested in accelerating its conclusion we have to be content to spend most of our lives incomplete, unfulfilled, imperfect. This means that we have to be prepared to accept that our present state is less than ideal without getting uptight or losing our nerve.

The road to ongoing conversion has its beginning in moments of self-questioning that are, in reality, invitations to growth. I am dissatisfied by my present reality because there is within me a burgeoning desire for something better. Perhaps we can define desire as *a sense of existential incompleteness.* I may not be able to pinpoint the feeling or name the object of desire since it is as yet unknown. I am aware only of a sense that my life lacks something, that I need to do something different with my life. At odd moments, I may say to myself, "There must be more to life than this." If these glimmerings of future possibility are ignored or rejected, then it is likely that my whole existence will become stale without my knowing why. I will probably lay the blame on circumstances or on other people, but the underlying cause of my lassitude is that I have failed to take up the option of growth when it appeared.

Most people who embrace a more intense spiritual life are at least idealists and, often enough, perfectionists. They may not have the clarity of vision that Abba Moses exhibits in Cassian's first *Conference*, but they begin the journey because they experience a formless aspiration for a more intense and focused life that will speed their steps toward God. To employ Abba Moses's terminology: purity of heart (personal integration) is their immediate goal, and God's transcendent kingdom their ultimate destination. The thing about goals is that they are goals, ideals are ideals, the end point of life's journey is reached only after a lifetime of traveling. This means that we are not there yet. Arriving at the place we want to be is our goal; it is what we are working to achieve, but it is for the future. For the moment, truth demands that we be somewhat dissatisfied with where we are. This dissatisfaction is the fuel that powers our desire and in fact is the energy source for meaningful living. The Latin term *desiderium* is a derivative of the verb *deesse*—to be absent. We cannot desire what we already possess; desire is the way love expresses itself when the object of its affection is absent.

The theme of desire for God is of great importance in patristic thought—we might think of Gregory of Nyssa and Augustine as prime proponents.[26] It is particularly significant in Western monasticism, as the title of Jean Leclercq's famous study of the culture of the medieval monastic world indicates: *The Love of Learning and the Desire for God*. Desire is an attractive word, but it is important that we do not allow our notion of what it signifies to become too lyrical. Desire is simply what we experience when something is missing. In Augustine's terms, it is the *rerum absentium concupiscentia*, the yearning for what is absent, the hankering after things we do not have.[27] Absence is the key component of desire.

Desire is like a springboard. We know our present departure point (what we have and what we are at the moment), but we do not know where we are going to end up. When we speak of desire for God we are not speaking of a desire that has a clear picture of its objective—it is merely the formless aspiration to move away from the present toward an unknown future. We are affirming that to the extent that we experience desire, God is absent from our lives. So, the object of spiritual desire is transcendent—it is beyond what eye can see or ear can hear or the human imagination can conceive. It is beyond all that we know or experience. We desire what is beyond. The paradox involved here is that this invisible reality has a dynamic power of attraction that has the effect of energizing us to search more deeply. It is not fantasy; it is not delusion. Its reality can be verified by the energy it imparts.

The presence of a nonspecific and unboundaried desire—even in an inchoate degree—indicates that at some level there has been an encounter with a reality that is beyond categories, something wholly other, the unconditioned, the Absolute. This is the *mysterium tremendum et fascinosum* to which Rudolf Otto drew our attention in his well-known study *The Idea of the Holy*.[28] The mystery that is God is fearsome and fascinating both. The beginning of the spiritual adventure is an unplanned, unsolicited, uncontrolled contact with spiritual reality, not known as an object but only by inference from the feelings aroused. It is like being suddenly wakened from sleep. We know that we are awake and that previously we were asleep, but we may not necessarily know exactly what prompted the transition from one state to the other. To reframe in terms of Friedrich Schleiermacher's perspective: there is a glimmer of a sense of ultimate or absolute dependence without there being a clear notion of the reality on which we are dependent.[29] To use another metaphor, much favored by the mystics, we are, as it were, suspended between heaven and earth; we have left earth behind but are still under the influence of its gravitational pull, and we have not yet set our feet in heaven—we are left hanging.[30]

It is worthwhile considering the Greek term *musterion*. For us a mystery is simply a puzzle—an unknown that invites further investigation. In antiquity, the word had a bit more substance. A "mystery" is something that is so full of reality that it cannot be spoken about, something about which silence must be maintained because even the loftiest language belittles its reality. It is a secret known only to initiates and hidden from outsiders. A spiritual experience is a mystery in the sense that it occurs in a kind of rational vacuum. There are no words or concepts that can convey what has happened.[31] Poetry and art try to express something of the mystery but can do no more than hint at its content. Its ultimate meaning escapes us. Our discourse can be no more than allusive.[32] The urgent desire to penetrate deeper into the mystery does not necessarily connect with the person's previous philosophy or their manner of living. It is, as we have noted previously, discontinuous. It seems to belong to a parallel universe.

What I am laboring here is the point that desire for God is unlike any other desires in that there is no clear perception of what is desired. On the surface, desire for God is experienced as a vague sense of dissatisfaction, discontent, even disenchantment. Its effect is a movement away from what we know in the direction of the Unknown. There is a feeling that there must be something beyond what fills my thoughts and ambitions at the present moment. The desire for God is experienced as the failure to be satisfied by anything else. According to the famous quotation from Augustine that many readers will recognize: "You have made us for yourself and our hearts are restless until they rest in you."

A glimpse of God can be powerful enough to change the way we live our lives. Note that there is a moral imperative inherent in desire for God. If we are to allow this desire to be translated into an active seeking after God, we must be prepared to give it precedence over other alternative sources of gratification: a desire that outweighs in importance all other desires.[33] To make desire for God the defining principle of our life involves a certain sobriety or austerity in the way we live. If there are those for whom even a strong spiritual experience seems to yield no fruit it is probably because they cannot cope with the dread associated with changing their lives. They are fearful of losing control. They do not want to face the prospect of giving up some of what presently makes their lives enjoyable. The fact is that most spiritual and mystical traditions place a certain emphasis on renunciation, particularly during the period of initial transition, but also in different modes throughout the whole spiritual life. To state the principle baldly: We cannot become wholeheartedly involved with the spiritual world if we are unwilling first to reduce our engagement with the world of space and time. At a later stage there may be a call to reengage with a view to evangelization, but first a break needs to be made.

Desire for God flourishes in the desert, although sometimes it makes a tentative—and perhaps unwelcome—appearance in a well-weeded garden. As human beings we have a tendency to accumulate whatever things seem good to us. This process of continual enrichment eventually becomes burdensome. We labor to procure what we think will satisfy us. Once we have it we find that, according to the song written by Irving Berlin, "After you get what you want you don't want it." And once we have what we sought in our hands, we fear to lose it. If we do lose it we grieve over our loss. Radical detachment may seem a demanding value, but it liberates us from the thralldom of possessions. You might remember another song, this time from the 1970s: "Freedom's just another word for nothing left to lose." If this is true of material possessions it also applies to other realities such as social standing, career opportunities, good health, mental acuity, entertainment and whatever is "highly esteemed among human beings." To find God we have to separate ourselves from what is not-God. This is the hard core of desire for God. If you want to take possession of the treasure hidden in the field you have to sell everything else to buy that field. It would be nice if there were an easier means of entering the kingdom, but there is no other way. The good news, however, is that usually we are able to make payments in installments. We don't lose everything at once. Furthermore, often enough we don't have to do anything to dispose of what we have; it is just taken away from us by some force majeure.

Detachment, as I have said previously, is less an action than a state. It is not so much a definitive act of giving up once and for all, but an ongoing condition of doing without. This means that deprivation loses any novelty value it may have had in the beginning. But what is happening is important. Voluntary renunciation leads us to the point of accepting a new identity. Instead of defining ourselves by what we had or what we did or according to how others saw us, we are led to a sense of who we are in our essential selves. Augustine is clear on this point: we are defined by what we desire. As spiritual desire begins to displace more biological and mundane desires we start to live a new identity.

A willingness or even an enthusiasm to take practical steps toward greater detachment is an ordinary sign that spiritual interest is authentic, and not merely a passing fad. New Age mysticism doesn't seem to demand much in the area of renunciation—it merely adds a bit of hocus-pocus without displacing anything in the status quo. A lot of the contemporary zest for distinguishing "spirituality" from "religion" seems to me to be a reluctance to yield individual autonomy—"self-will" in traditional terminology—to an organized entity outside ourselves that might make demands on us. Whatever rules such spirituality imposes, to the extent that it insists on anything, it leaves the bulk of life choices within the control of the self. There is no authentic self-transcendence.

Desire for God asks that it be given priority in our lives. It will never completely displace other desires, but it asks that we subordinate these passing fancies to what is most important and most permanent in our life. This is an example of the principle of *ordinatio caritatis* enunciated by Saint Augustine in his *City of God*:[34] we must impose some priorities on our affective tendencies so that we love more what is higher. The theme was further developed by the medieval Cistercians. We can never eliminate alternative affective movements or tendencies, but we can strive to subordinate them. This demands a certain clarity about the importance of the spiritual pursuit. I have to be able to say to myself in all sincerity: this is the most meaningful aspect of my life. My first priority is to seek God's kingdom; once that is settled I may learn to hope that all other necessities will be looked after.

In a cultural context that welcomes the so-called prosperity gospel, religious groups may be reluctant to include the idea of renunciation in their propaganda, but a certain austerity of lifestyle is an essential element of every life that is marked by dedication, and of any attempt to take seriously the call of the gospel. This is true not only at the beginning but throughout life. In some form or other, silence, solitude, community life, sobriety, chastity, humility, and moderation must be present. They are the means that enable us to focus more fixedly on the goal that led us to begin the journey. Without them our life becomes progressively more directionless. In traditional terms a purposeless life is said to be beset by the vice of *acedia*. The tendency to water down appropriate renunciation and austerity has been a perennial temptation even in monasteries. If ancient religious orders are much-reformed it is because they have repeatedly fallen into a state where reform is needed. There is always a danger of "a self-legitimating spiral of laxity," in which a group loses its focus, and begins to let things slide. Usually there are valid reasons for each downward step; the problem is that no note is taken of the cumulative effect of such mitigations. Challenge and comfort belong together; one without the other does not bring about long-term results. We need to be unashamed that our discipleship makes demands on us that we otherwise would have deemed unacceptable. As with everything else, the benefits are available only to those who pay their dues.

In the Augustinian tradition delight (*delectatio*) is the engine that drives our spiritual life forward, but for most of us such delight is an acquired taste. A withdrawal from immediate gratifications is the condition for the development of a certain sensitivity to spiritual realities: we have to cleanse our palate if we are to develop a true sense of the things of God. The challenge is that this reality of God is invisible, intangible, beyond our imagination. We have no clear and rational understanding of what we desire. The existence of the desire is the only piece of data we have. What we desire has to be inferred from the quality of the desire itself—and that is subject to evolution and change as our spiritual life progresses.

Progressively austerity moves from being an imposition toward something like an element in personal style, even a preference. As Saint Benedict notes at the end of his seventh chapter, fear and labor give way to love and delight; doing the right thing has become second nature (RB 7.68–69). This sobriety or austerity begins to envelop even the experience of prayer. As *The Cloud of Unknowing* insists, our interchange with God becomes so content-free that eventually it seems to disappear and all we are left with is "the naked intent," pure and unalloyed desire.

It is natural for prayer to become more apophatic, less reliant on the explicit content of words and concepts. Thomas Merton sums up this development well in a passage from the last book he wrote before he died.

Contemplative prayer is, in a way, simply the preference for the desert, for emptiness, for poverty. One has begun to know the meaning of contemplation when [one] intuitively and spontaneously seeks the dark and unknown path of aridity in preference to every other way. The contemplative is one who would rather not know than know. Rather not enjoy than enjoy. Rather not have *proof* that God loves him.[35]

This may seem a high ideal, and it is certainly beyond our powers to bring it about. We do not have to. It is a natural development of ordinary heartfelt prayer, taking place according to God's providence for each.

For Saint Bernard, this movement away from the tangible in the direction of the unknown is a summons to follow the ascended Christ into the heart of God. The following passage is a reminder that such a development—even when it is ardently desired—does not occur without a certain degree of malaise and complaint.

There are others for whom Christ has risen but not yet ascended. Indeed, he still remains with them on earth in holy sweetness. These are they who experience devotion all day, who weep in their prayers and sigh in their meditations and all things are for them a source of celebration and joy, and through all these days Alleluia is sung without interruption. But this milk must be taken away from them so that they may learn to be fed by solid food. It is *good* for them that Christ departs and that this temporal devotion be withdrawn. But when will they be capable of understanding this? They complain that they have been deserted by the Lord and deprived of grace. But let them wait a little. Let them remain sitting in the city while they are imbued with more solid virtue from on high and receive the greater gifts of the Holy Spirit.[36]

Desire operates at the level of affectivity and thus has an influence on the choices that we make. The way we intensify our desire is by allowing it to be translated into *seeking*. We give assent to the attraction we feel welling up within us. We actively put ourselves into the pursuit of the mysterious object of our desire. Whatever language we use to describe it, whether it be moralistic or mystical—as in the Song of Songs—at the heart of every genuine spiritual journey is a seeking of God. The question, "What are you seeking?" that Saint Benedict asks of a candidate for monastic life is one that we need to ask ourselves often in our lifetime. *Ad quod venisti?* (RB 60.3). When we lose sight of the goal we are likely thoughtlessly to go astray.

Abba Moses's discourse on the ultimate and proximate goals of monastic life is a good reminder of the eschatological character of any Christian life.[37] By whatever path we make our way, we all hope to attain a high level of personal integration so that our seeking is not subverted by subpersonal tendencies within us. And, in some form, we desire an end to the journey, we keep traveling because we want to arrive at our destination. What we experience here on earth will reach its culmination only in heaven. Much of the upset and confusion that have troubled us here below will begin to make sense as we get nearer to the end of our journey. Christian life will lack meaning if we do not take into consideration that it is designed as a road to eternal life. Its meaning is derived from arriving at its destination. Meanwhile there are many things that puzzle us as we make progress. It often seems that in the kingdom of God the normal laws of causality do not apply. At least at the level of appearances, there are causes without effects and effects without causes. What we are gambling on is that somehow everything will come together in God's own time. What is important is that through all the vicissitudes of life—by God's grace—we remain standing.

As soon as the eschatological note is sounded we hear the echo of another New Testament theme: staying awake, alert, vigilant. This implies remaining conscious of this fundamental desire by which we are led. The problem is that we are often distracted by more tangible desires, with more tangible incentives at the biological or social levels. I have to eat, I have to sleep, I enjoy working, I need affirmation. My day can be filled pursuing such goals. If what I am really seeking in life is merely a full stomach, a rested body, the employment of my talents, and the approval of others, then is there any time left for anything else? Probably not. This means some effort on my part to make time for what I am beginning to recognize as the most important activity in which I am engaged. It is useless to try to find time for spiritual exercises. There is no time to be found. I have to make time. This means that other desirable activities have to be left undone.

It is the time we devote to prayer that feeds our spiritual desire—if we are careful to impose a moratorium on alternative desires and enter into the desert. To leave other things aside for the moment to become more aware of what is less apparent amid all the comings and goings of daily activity. Patiently to sit in silence, swatting the distractions that seek to win our attention and accepting that what we are experiencing is an important part of the truth about ourselves. With regularity, even the dullest among us will begin to detect the faint stirrings of a yearning that is, perhaps, at odds with how we live. The next step is finding words that in some way encapsulate what we are feeling. Sometimes the Psalms can help to trigger a spasm of recognition. We will all have our favorite texts that seem to speak what we feel.

As the hind longs for the running waters,
So my soul longs for you, O God. (Psalm 41/42:1)

O God, you are my God, for you I long;
for you my soul is thirsting.
My body pines for you
like a dry weary land without water. (Psalm 62/63:1)

The more we exercise our desire in times of prayer, the more likely it will be that this ultimate yearning will begin to have an influence on the choices that we make and so, in the course of a lifetime, will be an agent of transformation in our lives. But let us note. Desire is often disguised: a generic, low-level dissatisfaction may, in reality, be a call to go higher, to upgrade. In life. In prayer. We need to learn to respond by asking questions of ourselves and inquiring of the Lord, who will show us the path of life, the fullness of joy in his presence.

Lord God,
You alone can satisfy the restless longings of the human heart.
Reveal yourself to us as you did in the burning bush,
Enflame our hearts and confirm our wills
Truly to seek you and sometimes to find you.
We ask this in the name of Jesus, the Lord.
Amen!

CHAPTER THREE

The Grace of Humanity

A t first glance the gift of humanity does not seem to be much of a thrill. We are certifiably human even before we are born—supposing we have the necessary forty six chromosomes that support our application to join the human race. Yet "humanity" is more than a zoological category—it is also a moral designator. We condemn people for being inhuman and praise them for their humanity. Here we are talking about attitudes, choices, and actions, not chromosomes. This leads us to conclude that perhaps our humanity is a work in progress, that there are degrees of humanity. In this case, the underlying purpose of all human development and also of the spiritual journey is to dismantle the obstacles to full humanity and to help us to grow toward a humanity that is more complete.

I have been saying for years that understanding the spiritual journey requires more than theology. It requires an equal measure of what we might term "spiritual anthropology." It is not enough to know about grace, to write a thesis on Augustine's theology of grace, to master all the twists, turns, and tangles of post-Reformation theology. We must also have a sympathetic understanding of the recipient of grace. We need to appreciate how the transcendent reality of divine grace interacts with the workaday reality of the human condition since, as the Scholastic theologians used to say, "Whatever is received is received in the measure of the receiver." Grace itself is limitless; any restrictions come from the side of the receiver, that is, from us. Grace as it is received is often less complete than grace as it is given.

Obviously, there are multiple interpretations of the human phenomenon, shaped by ideology, by methodology, and by the range of data surveyed to arrive at the conclusion. Since the human being is composed of opposite and sometimes conflicting elements, much depends on where we focus our attention. Do we begin with the human being as an amalgam of physical elements, as a product of animal evolution, or as an intelligent and spiritual being? We humans are all of these and, so, our self-understanding will be determined by which aspects of our complex reality we prioritize. For the picture to be complete we need to employ a dialectical method that aims at finding some common ground between the opposites, rather than excluding anything that complicates our facile picture of what constitutes our humanity.

I am not going to attempt to formulate a personal anthropology—that is far beyond my capabilities. What I would like to do is simply to evoke an approach to human reality that has had the most influence in the evolution of Christian spirituality. This is the vast reservoir of reflection that has been built up over the last two millennia that takes its starting point from the statement in Genesis that human beings were made in the image and likeness of the creating God. In his 1967 two-volume study of the theme as it occurred in the twelfth century, written in an era of pen and ink and typewriters, Robert Javelet notes that his research into more than one hundred authors of that century led to a collection of more than twenty thousand index cards.[38] Much of this subsequent reflection would, no doubt, have come as a surprise to the author of the biblical text. We are not talking here so much about exegesis. What we find is a great flowering of the theological imagination that takes its inspiration and language from Genesis and then tries to put into words its own intuitions concerning the essential meaning of human reality.

The foundational component of this traditional anthropology is that human reality must be interpreted within the context of God—desire for God is not merely a personal, or even an eccentric, choice but it is an ontological imperative. That means that an attraction to the invisible spiritual world is a consequence of what we are as humans. In this context, to deny this affective tendency is to distort humanity. Notwithstanding the gulf between temporality and eternity, there is no incompatibility between us and God—at least from God's side. A distance, but no unbridgeable chasm. Relationship with God exists, and it is possible for us to become conscious of it. Our connection with God preexists our awareness of being connected.

This is, fundamentally, a very positive picture of human reality. Our linkage with the spiritual world is the premise on which human dignity is predicated. In his 2015 book *Inventing the Individual: The Origins of Western Liberalism*,[39] Larry Siedentop has demonstrated—at least to my satisfaction—that the emphasis on the moral equality and dignity of all individuals has its ultimate roots not in the philosophy of classical Athens or Rome, nor in the eighteenth-century European Enlightenment, but in the New Testament. He asserts that the most credible source of the idea that all human beings enjoy an equality that is based on their shared nature is not something derived from philosophical inquiry, but that it has its origins in early Christianity. We would say, perhaps, that it is the result of divine revelation. Furthermore, he sees its most complete social embodiment of this ideal in a Benedictine monastery—possibly an imagined one, as distinct from historical examples. By living in practical accordance with gospel values we create an ambience that nurtures and sustains persons in their humanity. Evaluating every human person in the context of that person's nonmaterial component inevitably leads to a higher level of respect. The respect for human life in all its manifestations is an integral component of Christian faith. Some might extend this concept by including respect for all creation—animal, vegetable, and mineral—within its ambit. To the casual observer, those countries whose social structures have not been formed by Christianity seem to value individual human lives less—although that could simply be a projection from the eye of the beholder.

In the Cistercian authors of the twelfth century the theme of the image of God is developed into a whole spirituality, based on the principle of *noblesse oblige*.[40] If it is our nature to be images of God then our attitudes and behavior should also mirror the one in whose image we have been created. Here is a text from the late twelfth-century Cistercian treatise *The Interior House*.

> Understand your dignity, O noble creature, since you are not only endowed in the image of God but you are made beautiful by God's likeness. Just as your Creator who created you in his likeness is good and just, gentle and meek, patient and merciful with the other high qualities of which we read, so too you have been created so that you will have charity and be clean and holy, beautiful and elegant, meek and humble. The more virtues you have in yourself the closer you will be to God and you will manifest a greater likeness to your Creator.[41]

Note that the author seems to believe that we have an innate obligation to be "beautiful" and "elegant." Any failure in this department goes against what we were created to be. The word *dignity* is very important in the approach taken by the Latin church fathers in describing the human condition. Remember that such instances of inhumanity as slavery, the subjugation of women, tyranny, and horrific violence were constant features of societies at that time. It is against this background that we stand in admiration of the Christian leaders of late antiquity who dared to oppose the prevailing mind-set with the affirmation of the inalienable right of every human being to an existence that corresponded with the dignity of their spiritual nature.

Among the Cistercian writers there is what might be called an "ontological optimism," a sense of wonder and reverence for human reality as it has been created by God, combined with a confidence that God can bring to completion the good work that has been begun. Saint Bernard is constantly astounded by the thought of the vastness of the human soul. It is no trivial reality, but a capacity or potentiality created with a view to containing God.

> Oh, how great is the size of the soul and how amply endowed with merits it is, that it is sufficiently capacious and has been found suitable to receive the divine presence within itself! How large is that which can provide suitable broad avenues for His Majesty to walk along. Such a soul cannot afford to become involved in law suits and in other worldly cares and causes, nor to give itself over to the belly or to sex. It must leave aside idle entertainment, the will for universal domination and the pride which comes with power. For a soul to become a heaven and thus become the dwelling place of God, it must first ensure that it is empty of all these other things.[42]

Bernard, you will note, does not dwell long on the theoretical splendor of the soul; his instinct is to pass quickly on to its practical ramifications. He usually distinguishes between "image" and "likeness." "Image" is the fundamental and permanent state of compatibility with the divine: we always remain capable of a relationship with God. This is a universal human potentiality that is never lost. What we forfeited in the Fall was the "likeness"—the actualization of our potentiality for union with God. Our task, as he sees it, is to regain the "likeness" to God, step by step, in the course of a lifetime.

The Western Church has, perhaps, become too enmeshed in authoritarian attitudes in recent centuries to incorporate such insights into its commonplace practices, preferring to put the emphasis on conformity with social goals. I was reminded of how much is lost in such an approach when, in June 2003, a group of monastic formators visited a Buddhist monastery in Korea. There we were regaled with a long address from the abbot. The thing that struck me strongly at the time was his emphasis on self-realization, self-actualization. In his view, people come to monasteries in order to achieve their full potential; monastic discipline aims simply at removing the obstacles to this goal. It seemed to me that this was a far more attractive marketing tactic than what we find in most Christian recruitment literature. Perhaps we have placed too much emphasis on "seeking" rather than on "finding," on keeping the rules rather than on personal growth.

In his book *The Courage to Be*, Paul Tillich wrote, "It is time to end the bad theological usage of jumping with moral indignation on every word in which the syllable 'self' appears."[43] In many Christian circles "self" has come to be identified with "sin"—something to be monitored, restrained and, if possible, eliminated. A particularly virtuous person is described as "selfless." If you reflect upon it for a moment, this description is not so complimentary! If you think of some of the traditional lives of the saints or look at the featureless "holy pictures" that portrayed them, you might be excused for thinking that sanctity was a matter of being wishy-washy![44] By leaching out all the vices the virtues were left bland and colorless. This opened the way to seeing sanctity in terms of conformity with institutional expectations. The saints were those who didn't cause trouble, who kept the rule, minded their own business, and did what they were told. We forget that most real saints were not conformists, and probably caused many headaches for those over them. Perhaps we need to change our focus—for example, regarding obedience: our fundamental obligation is to *be* or to *become* what God wills. To *do* what God wills is secondary, depending on something more fundamental: action accords with being: we act according to what we are.[45] We serve God and profit the Church primarily by becoming the persons God intended us to be; in such a state doing God's will follows without much drama. Listen to what Parker Palmer wrote in his book *Let Your Life Speak: Listening for the Voice of Vocation*:

> Our deepest calling is to grow into our own authentic self-hood, whether or not it conforms to some image of who we *ought* to be. As we do so, we will not only find the joy that every human being seeks—we will also find our path of authentic service in the world.[46]

At the time of the much-watched wedding of Prince William and Kate Middleton, the celebrant, the Anglican bishop of London, surprised many by quoting Catherine of Siena—whose feast day it happened to be: "Become what you were meant to be and you will set fire to the whole earth."[47] Our first imperative is to be what God has created us to be, and everything else will flow from that.

At this point it is probably helpful to refer to an important distinction to which we will be returning later on. One of the key themes in the writings of Thomas Merton is the opposition between what he called, variously, the true self and the false self, the deep self and the superficial self, the inner self and the outer self. "Unless we discover this deep self, which is hidden with Christ in God, we will never really know ourselves as persons. Nor will we know God. For it is by the doors of this deep self that we enter into the spiritual knowledge of God."[48]

The whole point of this alternative view of humanity is to emphasize that we become more human by opening ourselves to the spiritual world, and we become less human by withdrawing from such contact. Our human nature has a spiritual or contemplative dimension: to ignore it is to debase ourselves. Spirituality is not merely a means of becoming more "spiritual." If it is genuine it should be a means of becoming more human, less inhuman, more humane. It is possible to fulfill all the statutory obligations of our state of life without developing on a personal level: putting in an appearance and punching the clock while the heart is far away from what is being done. If we were only to grow in mindfulness so that we could exploit the full potential of the things we do every day, our lives would soon be transformed. I suppose I am talking about a good zeal animating and guiding what we do rather than slavish conformity to rules and expectations, or to our own routines.

The bottom line has to be the conviction that religion or spirituality is not an optional extra to our humanity, but an integral and essential part. If you like Scholastic language, it is more a "formal" than a "material" element. It animates whatever we do rather than monopolizing the hours of the day. Salt adds savor to a food, but we would scarcely want to make a meal of salt on its own. Religion or spirituality is meant to enhance life, not to replace it. Otherwise we would be reserving holiness to a spiritual elite, professionals who do nothing else with their lives, rather than seeing it as an essential quality of God's faithful people—the little ones who are more adept at living the gospel than at preaching it. The significance of being created in the image of God is that there is a spiritual dynamism present in every human life, present even when it is latent. We will make good progress on our journey to God if we can recognize this energy and identify with it. Trying to manufacture our own plans for "a spiritual life" won't get us far, and when the novelty wears off we will probably abandon them. And just as well.

This philosophical view of the nature of humanity grounds an optimistic view of what we are and of what heights we are capable. But it needs to be tempered by a historical perspective. Yes, we read in the early chapters of Genesis that we were created in God's image, but read on! The Fall followed, then Cain and Abel, and then thousands of years of blood-stained human interaction. Including the Shoah, the Cultural Revolution in China, Stalin's purges, the killing fields of Pol Pot, Rwanda, Burma, the so-called Islamic State, sexual abuse and its toleration—and innumerable examples of crimes against humanity: inhumanity, antihumanity. Surely these too must enter into our understanding of what humanity is: what we are. As the Roman poet Terence memorably wrote: "I am a human being and nothing that belongs to humanity is foreign to me." If we are to live in truth, we cannot turn aside from the anti-human elements in our collective history or from the malicious tendencies that may sometimes influence the choices we make. Probably, most of us would have accepted employment as guards in a concentration camp—if our circumstances had been different. Such a step would have been simply the inevitable consequence of a long series of compromises, each one legitimated by the fact that it was hardly different from what went before. Perhaps the only thing that holds us back from crimes against humanity is a lack of opportunity. We are lucky that we have been born in a different era when we are not confronted by such dilemmas.

It may be, however, that neither theology nor history provides a positive response to the dark chapters of human malevolence, but only meta-history: the course of events in time and space as viewed from God's standpoint. Our temporal existence makes ultimate sense only in the context of the reality that lies beyond space and time and which is not directly accessible to rational analysis: God's saving plan. Our faith leads us to the conviction that there is an overarching Providence that is constantly at work, bringing all things to completion in Christ. The fact that we cannot see this or comprehend how this could be so does not mean that it is not happening. It simply means that the workings of Providence transcend our time-conditioned intelligence.

Look for example at the first chapter of the Epistle to the Ephesians: it is as though undergraduates staged a competition to cram as many technical terms as possible into a single sentence. The Greek sentence contains 203 words with (by my count) more than 40 words that merit specific commentary. It is an extraordinarily profound and yet moving overview of human history. This is how the sentence begins.

> Blessed be God the Father of our Lord Jesus Christ, who has blessed us in the heavenly places with every spiritual blessing in Christ, just as he chose us in him before the framing of the world to be holy and blameless in his presence, predestining us in love to be sons [and daughters] to him through Jesus Christ, in accordance with his pleasure and will—to the praise of the glory of his grace with which he gifted us in the Beloved, . . . (Eph. 1:3–6)

There are many indications that the real and permanent action in God's interaction with the world is taking place outside the spatiotemporal sphere. God does good things for us outside space (in the heavenly places), and outside time (before the framing of the world). All is predestined there is an anticipatory purpose (*pro-thesis)* to be put into complete effect only in the fullness of time. This text, in all its profundity, reminds us that God's action is not determined by what we do; it is not a response or reaction to our conduct, but it is divinely self-motivated. It is God's choice, made according to the good-pleasure of God's will, freely given and lavished, according to the counsel of that will. What God has done in creating us and in saving us has been done in total gratuity. And this is because the ultimate purpose is to generate the praise of God's glory. The way I understand "glory" is as a radiance, a revelation that precipitates spontaneous wonder or admiration in the being of the beholder: the ultimate attractive force that draws the percipient out of self in a movement of joyful ecstasy that is the culmination of human experience.

In a sense, we can define human reality in terms of its capacity to be brought to fulfillment by the vision of God. We were made with a view to our being able to say with Jacob after his wrestling bout with the angel: "I have seen God face to face and my soul has been saved."[49] God's will is that all will be saved and come to the knowledge of the truth. We were made to meet God, and it is in this encounter that we become simultaneously fully human and fully divine.

Lord Jesus Christ,
We have been made in your image,
And we are called to grow in your likeness.
Help us to become more like you
In innocence and compassion,
In patience and forgiveness,
In wisdom and love,
So that we may be a channel of your presence
to the world in which we live.
For you are our Lord for ever and ever.
Amen!

CHAPTER FOUR

The Grace of Alternation

I n our first chapter, we made the point that the advent of grace often takes the form of an interruption to "business as usual"—the grace of discontinuity. Of course, we resent this because it precipitates us into a state of wrong-footedness. We prefer to deal with predictable challenges. In real life this rarely happens. Often, our defenses, like the supposed guns of Singapore in 1942, are all pointing in the wrong direction. The enemy refuses to attack us in the manner we had anticipated and sneaks up on us from behind. It's not fair!

It is one of the original contributions of Saint Bernard of Clairvaux to make clear that the default state of human consciousness is neither positive nor negative, but a combination of both states in succession.[50] Life is not all love, peace, happiness, and joy. Nor is it loneliness, upset, sadness, and gloom. The normal human being has experience of both conditions. To wish to exclude one dimension—the negative—would be to deform humanity. Would we credit William Shakespeare with such a profound understanding of the human heart if he had written only the comedies and not the tragedies as well? The asses' bridge that many of us balk at crossing is the realization that negative experience is a normal part of human life. The book of Job and the psalms of lamentation are not aberrations. Being human necessarily involves suffering.

Eastern European philosophers are more acutely aware of this because of centuries of experience; their outlook is quite different from the happy-face philosophy of Disneyland that is so popularly marketed in the West. For many of us happiness is seen as just another commercial product that can be purchased with the minimum of personal effort. In the perverted world of mass advertising, an unhealthy meal full of fats and sugar is a "happy meal." Happiness has become commodified. No attention is paid to the drama necessary to purge ourselves of the innate obstacles to authentic happiness and the unavoidable suffering that we all encounter sometimes. The Romanian philosopher Emil Cioran has written that suffering is the most universal human experience and therefore it deserves a place at the heart of philosophical inquiry. In the art of suffering we are all professionals. If negative experience is normal, then it is also right and just; it must serve a purpose: in which case, it is also good. If something feels bad it is because often it is pushing us out of our comfort zone and enabling us to grow into something new, beyond our self-imposed limitations. This becomes self-evident after a moment's reflection, but it is not so easy to market this truth to those who are affronted at the negativities they are forced to endure. The inevitable experience of tough times can make people doubt the soundness of their decision to begin the journey to look for a more abundant life.

The complexity of human nature and our tendency to be simultaneously pulled in opposite directions was recognized by the Second Vatican Council in its decree *On the Church in the Modern World*.

[The human being] is the meeting point of many conflicting forces. In our condition as a created being we are limited by a thousand shortcomings, yet we feel unlimited in our yearnings and destined for a higher life. Torn by a welter of attractions we are compelled to choose between them and to reject some of them. Worse still, feeble and sinful as we are, we often do the very thing we hate and do not do what we want. And so we feel ourselves divided and the result is a host of discords in social life.[51]

This text points to the importance of formulating a dialectical spirituality, one that does justice to the complexity of human being and human experience. Whether we embrace some form of the "prosperity gospel" or prefer a cult of victimhood, our life will be impoverished by the exclusion of the contrary principle. In particular, it is delusional to think we can continue going forward without any faltering or backsliding. It is a moral version of the nineteenth-century myth of progress so beloved of school mottoes and exemplified in Henry Ford's assembly line: "Onwards and upwards and never backward!" and "Every day and in every way to get better and better." Apart from the banality of the sentiment, it flies in the face of experience. If things kept getting better, we would surely reach a point where we could not take it anymore and we would burst.

Our precarious virtue, the effect of the weakness of our wills, is matched by the wobbliness of our intellect when it comes to grasping the highest spiritual truths. As Saint Augustine wrote,

Whoever judges that in this mortal life human beings may by our own action remove the fog of bodily and carnal fantasies so as to drink of the serene light of changeless truth with a mind habitually free from the ways of this life so that we may adhere to it with extraordinary and unswerving constancy of spirit, such a one understands neither what we seek nor the one who seeks it [*nec quid quaerat, nec quis quaerat*].[52]

We find it hard to correspond perfectly with God's plans for us and for the universe because our minds are too feeble to understand them. Not only is God beyond our comprehension; we have only a fragmentary and partial knowledge of ourselves and of human nature and even of the physical universe. We are easily distracted and, mostly, we prefer to be entertained than to be informed, to be spoon-fed rather than encouraged to think things through for ourselves.

The spiritual journey is not a trivial exercise that can be explained in a few clichés and mastered with minimal effort, safely quarantined from our normal everyday living. The spiritual journey is like a road that goes from somewhere to nowhere. We know our starting point, but we see our destination only dimly; there needs to be a certain tentativeness in deciding whether movement in a particular direction will lead me closer to where I want to be. Again, it is an example of the Dunning-Kruger effect, which we saw in chapter 1. Too much confidence that we have found the way is probably an indication that we are off the track but lack the intelligence to perceive it. Our uncertainty of intellect needs not only the compensation of a resolute will but also the correctives offered by being part of collective search for God that spans many centuries and is not limited to what is perceptible from our own insignificant location in time and space. Even after a lifetime of pondering the great mysteries of faith, I would be deluded to assume that everything about which I read is within my comprehension. My intimate and personal faith needs to be supplemented by a faith in the community of believers where others may be found who understand and put into practice what its beyond my capability.

When we seek God, even the God of revelation, even God, the Father of our Lord Jesus Christ, we are dealing with a *mysterium tremendum et fascinosum*—to use the phrase formulated by Rudolf Otto. God is both fearsome *and* fascinating; this is to say that both fear and love, flight and attraction, are appropriate responses. As Alfred North Whitehead wrote in *Religion in the Making*: "[Religion] runs through three stages, if it evolves to its final satisfaction. It is the transition from God the void to God the enemy, and from God the enemy to God the companion."[53] It is the middle phase, where God is perceived as an enemy, as One who does not conform to our own perceptions and plans, that is crucial. We have to change, we have to be converted, before a real relationship with God can begin. Sometimes this may mean frightening us out of our complacent dullness, though there is usually a carrot with the stick. Look through the pages of the Bible and you will find that accounts of theophanies manifest both tendencies. From the fig leaves of Adam and Eve to the terror of Moses, through the dread occasioned by the prophetic vision to the flight of Jonah and the cry of Simon Peter, "Depart from me for I am a sinful man," the encounter with the sacred inspires a kind of holy terror. A sense of not being good enough for the occasion. Unworthiness. Sometimes the best evidence for the authenticity of a spiritual experience is a frantic tendency to run as fast as possible in the opposite direction.

The fear and love we experience are the effects of the complementary qualities revealed in God's self-manifestation. Both are necessary for a balanced spiritual life. Saint Bernard speaks about mercy and judgment as being the two feet of God, by which he walks around the minds of those devoted to him.

It has sometimes been granted to a poor man like myself to sit at the feet of the Lord Jesus and, according to the condescension of his kindness, I have embraced now one foot and now the other. And if it happened that I became forgetful of his mercy and, driven on by conscience I clung too long to the foot of judgment then, at once, I was cast down by an unbelievable fear and by misery and confusion. I was surrounded on all sides by a terrifying darkness and was able only to cry out in fear from the abyss: "Who understands the power of your anger and fears the strength of your fury?" But if I leave the foot of justice and cling more tenaciously to the foot of mercy, I become slack, negligent, uncaring, tepid in prayer, slothful in deed, ready to laugh and not circumspect in conversation. The result is that both states of such a one are more lacking in stability than they should be. But since I have been instructed by the experience of my master (the Psalmist), it is not judgment alone or mercy alone, but both together which will be my song. I will not forget your just decrees and both mercy and judgment will be my song in this place of pilgrimage, until the time comes when mercy is lifted above judgment. Then unhappiness will be silent and my glory will sing to you without complaint.[54]

The double action of judgment and mercy and its effect in fear and confidence or boldness bespeak a double action for our amendment: comfort and challenge. "Learn from this that a twofold help can be expected from above in the spiritual task, namely, correction and consolation."[55]

More significantly, the variation in our experience is the result of our own innate state of interior division. Many authors appropriate to themselves what Saint Paul writes in the seventh chapter of the Epistle to the Romans concerning the unbaptized. There is a constant inner struggle. This inherent dichotomy is also apparent in the postexilic rabbinic teaching about the two *yetserim* (inclinations or tendencies) that seek to influence our choices. Following the Epistle of James (1:8 and 4:8), early Christian authors used the expression *dipsuchia* to indicate the state of having a double soul—being pulled in two directions at once. This is the default condition of every human being. The proximate goal of our active spiritual endeavors is to reduce this interior conflict, to attain—by God's grace—some measure of spiritual freedom, of singleness or purpose, for which the ancient monks used the term "purity of heart," *puritas cordis*.[56] It is extremely unlikely that we will be motivated to heal this inner rupture unless we are aware of it—painfully aware of it. If we insist on remaining in a state of denial, projecting all our problems and difficulties onto adverse circumstances or onto others then our "spiritual life" will almost certainly stagnate.

Bernard uses the terms *alternatio* (alternation) and *vicissitudo* (changeableness) to describe this aspect of human and spiritual life. His descriptions of it often begin with the clause *necesse est* (it is necessary). This variability is not primarily an effect caused by something we have done or failed to do, but must be viewed as the manifestation of the state in which our fallen nature exists. There is no avoiding it. To live in the truth means embracing both ends of the spectrum: it means recognizing, as Martin Luther would say, that we are simultaneously sinners and people who have been justified: *simul peccator et iustus*.

> For people who are spiritual, or rather, for those whom the Lord intends to make spiritual, this process of alternation goes on all the time. God visits by morning and subjects to trial. The just man falls seven times, and seven times gets up again. What is important is that he falls during the day, so that he sees himself falling and knows when he has fallen and wants to get up again and calls out for a helping hand saying, "O Lord, at your will you made me splendid in virtue, but then you turned away, and I was overcome."[57]

Mysteriously, when we fall, we fall into the hands of God. Whatever happens in life happens within the boundaries of divine providence—it is all provided for in God's plan for our salvation. The ups and downs of normal human life can be a source of grief for us if we are seeking to remain in control. We can easily be upset if we think that because our experience has changed, God's good opinion of us has faltered. "This is what causes my grief, that the way of the Most High has changed" (Ps. 77:10).

The experience of human variability can be transposed to the level of the interpersonal so that our ups and downs are interpreted as signs of God's presence or absence. It is important that this variation between positive and negative, between perceived presence and presumed absence, is interpreted in terms of a divine strategy to bring about our growth by augmenting our desire.

> Do you not see that those who walk in the Spirit can, in no way, remain for long in one state? One does not always make progress with the same facility. This is because one's ways are not one's own. They are moderated by the Spirit according to his plan: Sometimes progress is slower and, at other times, it is fast.[58]

Our lives are "moderated by the Spirit"—thankfully they are not totally under our control. If a sense of dependence on God is the essential component of all religion, then most of us have to be forced to discover and rediscover this dependence by getting ourselves into situations from which we cannot escape unaided. We need to be saved. Self-salvation is a contradiction in terms. But there is more to salvation than being plucked out of mortal danger. Every act of salvation is also an act of revelation. We come to an experiential knowledge of God by being saved by God. Salvation is the quintessential act of God's self-revelation. And there is something else. Through being saved we learn something fundamental about God, but also we are taught something about ourselves. If we lack the capacity to make a mess of our lives we will lack the possibility of being saved, and, because of this, we will never arrive at a personal knowledge of God and our self-knowledge will be defective.

> God makes himself known for our salvation through such an experience and it follows this order. First of all, one perceives oneself to be in dire straits, then one cries to the Lord and is heard. And then he will say "I will free you and you shall honor me." So, in this way, self-knowledge is shown to be a step in the direction of knowledge of God.[59]

Most of us can handle the good times easily enough. The question both for those whom we try to help and, more especially, for ourselves concerns how to respond when the going gets tough. Sometimes we find ourselves midwinter and insufficiently clad, when the best we can hope for in our prayer and in our commitment is "routine"—although, if we are not vigilant, it tends to slide down the scale toward "drab," "unexciting," and even vaguely hostile. We need to take a step back to look at our lives. Is the discomfort the direct result of choices that I have made? Have I allowed my life to become directionless? Is there a social component in my malaise that needs investigation and, perhaps, resolution? Am I tired, irritable, distressed, depressed, disenchanted? Am I reluctant even to address the situation? Perhaps the source of my discomfort can be tracked down and steps taken to relieve it. On the other hand, perhaps there is nothing wrong with me—I am just passing through a transitional phase when the initiative is taken away from me and God allows others to act on me to produce the desired result.

It is here that a little bit of theory can be eminently practical. We will handle negativity better if we are convinced that it is an unavoidable element in every human life and in every spiritual journey. The fact that we have become aware that something is wrong does not mean that something is wrong—there is something very right in our becoming aware of our situation. This means that if we cannot deal with it—as often we can't—then we have to endure it, and, as the New Testament reminds us, endurance builds character, for it is by patience in sharing Christ's cross that we are rendered more worthy of participating in his kingdom.[60]

It is here that we are confronted with the challenge of stability, which was the quintessential value and virtue for Saint Benedict.[61] What stability asks of us is that we stay with the process—even though this course of action is counterintuitive, even though everything seems to be going wrong. We must allow the cycle to complete before making a decision. The same is true for us throughout our lives. Sometimes we have to tough it out until things improve. Euthanasia is no remedy for the pangs of childbirth; we have to let things take their course. We may very well rebel interiorly. We can, however, be reasonably sure that reaching the goal of the spiritual journey is unlikely to be exempt from many frustrations and disappointments along the way.

What is asked of us is that we keep standing amid all the storms and whirlwinds. Standing is not sitting. Stability does not involve resting on our oars, nor does it mean developing a routine and spending the rest of our lives on autopilot. The image I have of stability is that it is like surfing. All you have to do is to stand on a surfboard and let it take you forward. This sounds easy. The difficulty arises because the board is moving at the behest of wind and wave, and it takes a lot of energy and continual adjustment as the center of gravity changes and both board and rider are swept either to a successful conclusion or to an ignominious dumping. To keep standing is the only way forward, and it is not always as easy as it may look on television.

If we are looking for advice on how to keep standing, we can do no better than look at the well-known text of Ephesians 6:10–17.

> Finally, be strong in the Lord and in his mighty power. Put on the full armor of God so that you can take your *stand* against the devil's schemes. . . . Put on the full armor of God, so that when the day of evil comes, you may be able to *stand* your ground, and after you have done everything, to *stand*. *Stand* firm then, with the belt of truth buckled around your waist, with the breastplate of righteousness in place, and with your feet fitted with the readiness that comes from the gospel of peace. In addition to all this, take up the shield of faith, with which you can extinguish all the flaming arrows of the evil one. Take the helmet of salvation and the sword of the Spirit, which is the word of God.

If you are interested in maintaining your stability, that is to say, in persevering to the end, this text gives some indicators: truth, righteousness, and a readiness to accept the gospel of peace. Also, faith, salvation, and the word of God. What it seems to be saying is that the ordinary means of living a good life, the everyday virtues, are self-maintaining. Drift away from these key elements of Christian discipleship and your hold on your commitment will gradually weaken. There is nothing particularly glamorous about gospel living, but this is not to say that it is without difficulty or challenge. There is always the danger that we will take our eye off the goal and allow ourselves to be drawn away from the path that leads to where we want to go.

Drift away we certainly will at some stage in our life, and probably more than once. This is where stability takes the form of resilience—the ability to bounce back after a major calamity. "Resilience is the capacity of individuals, communities, companies and the government to withstand, respond to, adapt to, and recover from disasters." Resilience grows out of sustained commitment to four factors: robustness (the ability to keep standing), resourcefulness (skillful management of the disaster), rapid recovery (getting back to normal quickly), and learning lessons from whatever happened. I note "robustness." A certain toughness is an important quality for any who would pursue the spiritual path.[62]

Change—external and internal—must be taken as the new normal; "Joy gives way to sorrow" (Prov. 14:13). Such alternation must not only be endured but also recognized as an important agent in our ongoing spiritual progress. Just as when we sleep we toss and turn alternately to exercise and rest different groups of muscles, so the variation we experience within and without enables us to develop complementary qualities that will lead to a much richer personality and a much deeper discipleship by the time we come to the end of our journey. Saint Bernard summed up his philosophy in a letter to Pope Innocent II in 1134.

> If sadness were our continual state, who could bear it? If, on the other hand, things always went well, then who would not think little of them? Wisdom, the careful controller of all things, alternates the temporal life of his chosen ones with necessary changing between good things and bad. By such a regimen, they will neither be crushed by adversity nor lose discipline through too much joy. Also, it is by this means that joys are more appreciated and difficulties more readily endured. Blessed be God forever![63]

Lord Jesus Christ,

You have called us to remain as your disciples

Through many changes and reversals of fortune.

Give us the grace of stability

So that we may continue in fidelity to you,

Faithfully following you in this life

So that we may, one day, follow you into the life that has no end.

Lord Jesus Christ, you are our Lord, for ever and ever. Amen!

CHAPTER FIVE

The Grace of Temptation

Temptation is something that most of us imagine we could happily do without. Yet Saint Aelred begins one of his talks to his monks with a quotation of James 1:12, "Blessed are those who endure temptation."[64] In fact, he considers temptation as the principal zone in which the monk is called to engage in spiritual warfare. The presence of temptation is an indication that everything is going well; its absence may be a cause for alarm. Temptation makes visible the radical dividedness of the heart; that may be unwelcome news, but it is better to know about it than not!

> The devil does not care about tempting a person whom he has already in his power. The devil has no care to approach those who obey their own concupiscence in all things and satisfy the desires of their flesh; but if they begin to throw off their concupiscences and struggle against the desires of their flesh, then the devil is grieved and he comes forward with a sharper attack.[65]

In Aelred's view temptation is not primarily about trying to get us to engage in some forbidden activity for its own sake. Temptation keeps battering against our weakest defenses not only in the hope of a breakthrough, but with the overriding purpose of making us discouraged. The underlying purpose is to damage our self-esteem and, so, to make us less confident and more tentative.

The spiritual warfare evident in temptation is a war of attrition. If we give in, we become discouraged. If we resist, we become fatigued with the fight—and discouraged. The symbolic meaning of temptation is that it reveals the dividedness of our own wills: we are not as good as we thought. Perhaps we begin to feel like hypocrites, professing a high ideal yet constantly living on the brink of succumbing to vice. Temptation may well be a means of making progress in self-knowledge and truth, but it wears us down and wearies us and causes a notable reduction in our joie de vivre. In some cases, people lose their nerve and go off to seek an easier path. For others it is more a matter of imposing such rigid standards on themselves that they make their lives a misery. As far as the devil is concerned this is mission accomplished.

If we are to begin to cope mentally and emotionally with the reality of temptation and the inner division it indicates, we may well need a refresher course in spiritual anthropology—looking at the way our alternation of experience is explained. We will cope much better if we understand what is going on.

In considering this situation, it is useful to draw on the ancient wisdom of monastic writers such as Evagrius of Pontus and John Cassian. They understood that there are resident vices present in every human soul, pre-elective tendencies that lead us away from God and, more importantly, cause us to become discouraged and to lose faith in the possibility of attaining close friendship with God. These tendencies result in temptation sneaking up on us, especially when we are low. They inject disturbing images into our imagination and unwelcome thoughts into our minds. As Saint Augustine wrote,

> Our life here in this time of journeying cannot be without temptation, for it is through temptation that we make progress and it is only by being tempted that we come to know ourselves.[66]

These vicious tendencies are mercifully concealed from us at the beginning of our spiritual journey. It is a sign of progress when we begin to be aware of them. It means that our powers of perception are becoming stronger. When we become aware of our contrary inclinations they lose their capacity to influence our choices subliminally. We can fight against them. This is the principal task of our spiritual warfare, one that will occupy us for most of our lives as disciples of Christ—from some time after the beginning until not long before the end. We remember the striking statement in Mark 1:13 concerning Jesus's temptation: "He was with the [wild] beasts and the angels ministered to him." Perhaps it is true also of us that we will not experience the ministry of angels until we have consented to confront the wild beasts within us; only then will we hear the divine response, "My grace is enough for you: power is made perfect in weakness" (2 Cor. 12:9).

From the time of Origen these innate vices were seen to be symbolized by the various tribes with which the people of Israel had to contend from the time of their departure from the dark slavery of Egypt until their arrival at the Promised Land. For Origen, these enemies were indwelling spirits or demons; his view was almost mythological. Evagrius took the understanding a step forward; he rebranded the demons in psychological categories, and they were designated as "evil thoughts." John Cassian saw them in moral or behavioral terms and so classified them as "vices," and, finally, Gregory the Great simply termed them "sins"—resulting in the list of what we know as the seven deadly sins. Gregory saw them as offenses against God, and hence his approach was more theological. By submitting to these natural tendencies we set ourselves against God's law. These are different ways of viewing the same universal human experience.

These eight primordial tendencies were listed as gluttony, lust, avarice, anger, sadness, acedia, vainglory, pride. If these designations seem to refer to realities outside our experience we can add some of their cousins: envy, sloth, contentiousness, mendacity, violence, flattery, ambition, substance abuse, exaggerated need for entertainment, overuse of social media, radical individualism, and many more. We could go on at some length listing vices together with their subcategories—just as the old manuals of moral theology used to do—and still miss the point. The main problem with the vices is not so much that they are objective or verifiable evils, but that they are obstacles to our journey toward God. They are barriers between us and God. Yes, the actions that stem from them may be objectively and perhaps intrinsically evil, but the main damage that they wreak is interior to the one who is seduced by them. Not only do they cut us off from making contact with God, they also effectively block our progress toward self-actualization. They do this, as we have already noted, by leading us away from the truth of our dependence on God into untruth. By disheartening us they make us reluctant to spend energy in extricating ourselves from their grasp. As a result of sin we feel unclean, lost, and psychologically burdened—to use the three major images of sin distinguished by Paul Ricoeur.

The approach to human reality that takes the vices as given, as something normal and innate, is no more than an expansion of the suggestion attributed to Jesus in the seventh chapter of Mark's Gospel. In response to criticism of his disciples' behavior Jesus points out that morality is far deeper than matters of ritual and taboo. An action is good or bad according to the personal content inherent in the action: motivation, intention, goodwill. These are what matter.

> And when [Jesus] entered the house away from the crowd, his disciples asked him about this parable. And he said to them, "Are you so lacking intelligence? Do you not understand that nothing entering into a person from outside can profane? For it does not go into the heart but into the stomach, and thence it goes out into the sewer." (Thus declaring

all foods pure.) He said that: "What comes out of a person is what profanes. For from within, out of a person's heart, come evil thoughts, fornications, thefts, murders, adulteries, acts of greed, and acts of malice; [from within come] deceit, lewdness, the evil eye [envy], slander, arrogance, and stupidity. All these evils come from inside and profane a person."[67] (Mk. 7:17–23)

The human heart is resistant to truth and goodness because of some kind of intrinsic defilement. Jesus speaks first of actions (the nouns are in the plural), then of tendencies or vices (with nouns in the singular). Jesus does not pussyfoot around these ugly manifestations of fallen human nature; he speaks plainly: it is vice, not food or "dirt" that profanes; the source is not some external taboo that has been violated but what sallies forth from the human heart.

Life-changing religion cannot remain at the level of appearance; a conversion to reality is required—including that part of reality that may be unknown, unconscious, or unseen. In this perspective, the virus of human malice cannot be cured by external poultices, though these may be a source of comfort. It demands a more radical and internal violence. "The human heart is devious from youth" (Gen. 6:5). "The heart is deceitful above all things and beyond cure. Who can understand it?" (Jer. 17:9). The human heart is the source of evil acts repeated often, resident vices, defilement. All upward movement must begin at the level of human depravity, recognizing what is in need of repair. As the poet W. B. Yeats declared, "I must lie down where all ladders start, / In the foul rag-and-bone shop of the heart."[68] Nothing permanent can be built on a mere facade of niceness. We need to acknowledge our vicious tendencies and the external acts that they have prompted in the past and, even now, continue to urge upon us. These vices preexist their expression (whether internal or external); they are universal. When (under grace) we subdue one, another pops up. And, it seems, we are never totally free of any: a residue remains; the ashes can burst into flame at any unguarded moment. Evagrius insists that such tendencies are not within our power and not fundamentally of our own creation, although we can encourage their growth by giving them free rein to influence our choices: "Whether or not we are troubled by all these [thoughts] does not depend on us. We may however be able to choose whether to prolong them and whether they move us or not."[69]

A passion or a spontaneous feeling is not blameworthy; it is a burden to be borne—it becomes malign only when free choice gives its assent, for example, when the feeling of anger is transformed into acts of aggression or the feeling of lust gives birth to acts of adultery. But all of us have to be prepared for temptation whether at the beginning of the journey or the end. As Saint Aelred warned his monks: "It is written, however, 'Son you have come to the service of God. Stand bravely and prepare your soul for temptation' (Sir 2:1). Immediately the affections for sins, the memory of delights, and long-lasting habit attack the poor soul from every side and cause it trouble."[70] Denial of our interior division leads to a delusory optimism about our spiritual status; we begin to believe our own self-exculpating rhetoric.

A refusal to admit the possibility of temptation and an unwillingness to perceive the malice of what it suggests lead eventually to what is termed in the New Testament "hardness of heart." This is an unperceived resistance to grace and to God, and thence, ultimately, involves a loss of humanity. Here is the beginning of a poem by Mary Oliver:

> Oh, the house of denial has thick walls
> and very small windows
> and, whoever lives there, little by little,
> will turn to stone.[71]

Insulating ourselves from reality makes us ever more impervious to the truth; eventually we turn to stone.

There are five chief aspects of hard-heartedness, used in the biblical sense. They are partly moral (the result of choices in the past or the present), and partly psychological, and, perhaps, partly the result of the social conditioning to which we have been exposed. Hardness of heart, in the biblical sense, is not primarily harshness or meanness in dealing with others. It is more a matter of impermeability, building impregnable defenses against the whole truth and thereby against ordinary humanity and even against God's loving mercy.

1. *Forgetfulness of God*: Lives lived without the conscious presence of God are either totally dominated by social conditioning or enclosed within the stout wall of self-will and self-counsel. Those who are a law unto themselves are not only isolated from the challenge of self-transcendence but also deprived of the comfort that makes the acceptance of challenge feasible. Nothing is allowed by way of feedback that may have the potential to threaten the status quo. There is no objective standard against which to measure ourselves. Self-indulgence and every vice are denied, rationalized, projected onto others. A large measure of generic blame is kept in storage for a rainy day: to become available to cover every contingency. Nothing that goes wrong is ever attributed to self. As a result, there are no absolute standards against which their choices may be measured. Morality is reduced to being a matter of personal or social convention. When God is excluded, the way is open to all kinds of undesirable effects. In his address accepting the 1983 Templeton Prize for Religion, Aleksandr Solzhenitsyn summarized the causes of the

tragedies and crimes of the twentieth century in the words of a Russian folk saying. "Men have forgotten God: that is why all this is happening."[72]

2. *Compensatory Attachments:* When God is excluded from life, people are forced to build their character and their careers around alternative centers. For some this means a relentless pursuit of power, possessions, pleasure, or privilege. For most in the Western world it is leads to superficiality. Too uninterested to profess atheism, many become woolly agnostics with a reluctance to commit themselves to anything beyond the ephemeral causes that temporarily hold their attention. Nearly half a century ago, the Israeli sociologist Shlomo Giora Shoham defined this attitude in terms of the ancient notion of acedia.[73] A butterfly attitude to life seems, at first glance, to be carefree and unrestrained, but in fact it is often enslaved by an addiction to entertainment.[74] This reality is evoked in the title of a book by Neil Postman: *Amusing Ourselves to Death.*[75] The circuses provided by social media may seem to make life worth living but, in reality, they are simply means of filling time—or killing time—without ever having to come to grips with the important and significant issues we face. So immersed are we in the frivolities of the virtual world that we fail to notice what is happening around us. The pursuit of trifles blunts the capacity to see reality and progressively incapacitates the spiritual faculties. For example, the hours spent plotting the rise and fall of celebrities—those who are famous because they are famous—can mean that we never spend much time reflecting on what is truly important. As Saint Bernard warned long ago, "The seeking after frivolous things amounts to contempt for the truth and contempt for the truth is the cause of our [spiritual] blindness."[76] We become unable to read "signs of the times"; we do not hear

the Spirit's voice calling out to us. As a result, our actions manifest a total insensitivity to the feelings and unspoken messages of others. We lack empathy and compassion and cannot even understand what these words signify. In such a scenario, we become less human and less alive.

3. *Lack of Self-Knowledge*: If an exaggerated concern for outward things uses up all our energy, we become strangers to our own inner world. Spiritual illiteracy means that we cannot read what is happening within and, so, we are unable to respond to the action of God in the soul—the stirrings of the Spirit—and, often enough, we do not quite understand why we act as we do. Even if residual religion remains a part of our lives it ceases to operate at the level of experience and becomes either a code of conventional morality or an intellectual system of prefabricated metaphysics. It is not surprising that, thus reduced, religion passes by seamless stages from meaningless routine to total abandonment—whether this be expressed by complete lack of interest in things spiritual or by active hostility. In the meantime, any appreciation of our own spiritual nature or our ultimate destiny fades away.[77]

4. *Lack of Self-Acceptance*: Where self-knowledge is defective, there can be no true self-love, which serves as the basis of our love for neighbor. Unconscious self-hatred inevitably leads to a distaste for others; we project onto them the unlovable aspects of ourselves that we repress. Not everybody so affected becomes a sociopath, but their relationships tend to become less other-centered, more self-serving and exploitative. The negative feedback received from such defective relationships only intensifies self-rejection and so can lead to a spiraling self-destructiveness. In some situations, a compulsive pursuit of intimacy follows, as the person seeks the lost self in the other, forcing the other to yield tokens of

esteem that are fake and undeserved. Without appropriate self-acceptance, what passes for love can become completely insensitive to the other's needs and desires, often resulting in violence toward the other and great unhappiness for both. In the light of this, the increase in incidents of domestic violence in Western societies can be seen for what it is, a cancer that requires urgent attention.

5. *Loveless Life*: A life without authentic love is barely human. Often, especially when lovelessness is combined with a pseudo-religious stance, it makes the person rigid, judgmental, lacking in natural kindness and compassion, unfair—as the typical Pharisee is portrayed in the Gospels. A life without self-giving love is marked by high and low individualism (*singularitas*), a relentless search for external goods (*cupiditas*), and an inability to commit to serious matters (*curiositas*). It leads to a loneliness, skepticism, cynicism, and many other dehumanizing and misery-making attitudes. Maybe we have met people like this.

"Who can soften hardness of heart? Only the grace of God. Human effort is not worth much here, as daily experience teaches us."[78] To become aware of our defenses is the first step in being able to consider dismantling them, to learn how to allow other people to get through to us, to let God get through to us. And this process can be begun by very simple steps. Pope Francis has suggested that our life together would be very much enhanced if we practiced saying three words: "please," "thanks," and "sorry." Maybe also, "Good morning." We might add yet another magic mantra: "I was wrong." This is one way we can dismantle some of the walls that divide the human family and try to build bridges instead. If we attempt to block out the bad, we will end up blocking out everything and condemn ourselves to living in radical isolation from others. Opening doors and windows and allowing ourselves to be vulnerable may well be the first stage in being able to recognize the wonderful things God is doing around us and in us. By God's grace we may proceed from there to the point of gratefulness and thanksgiving.

Temptation is not temptation unless it has a reasonable chance of success. And the most complete success is when temptation sneaks in unobserved and takes over the government. In this way, without much opposition, its suggestions become the default manner of acting and reacting. Individual actions merge into repetitive patterns of behavior: each success makes future successes more likely. Hardness of heart makes it less likely that we become aware of what is happening in our lives; we are too involved with matters of considerably less importance.

We are all tempted because all of us alike are involved in spiritual warfare. This means that we need to be prepared to accept casualties; fundamentally we are engaged in a war of attrition. It is not enough to cultivate the delusion that we can avoid sin; we need to develop attitudes and strategies to deal with situations in which we have succumbed to temptation. This means trying to view our fallen state through the eyes of God.

> While we are in this body we must flee from the face of the temptation that pursues us. And if sometimes we flee less swiftly then temptation catches us and we are knocked over, but the Lord catches us. . . . It is necessary, while we are detained in this world, that we will fall sometimes; but some stay down, others do not. . . . "The just fall seven times a day." There are different kinds of falls. When the just fall they are caught by the Lord and so they rise again, stronger than before. But when the unjust fall, there is no one to help them rise again. For they fall either into a harmful shame or into hardness of heart. They may offer excuses for what they did and thus shame leads them deeper into sin. Or they

show a bold face, like a prostitute, to indicate that they fear neither God nor human beings but, instead, like Sodom, they publicize their sin. The just, however, fall into the hand of God and in a marvelous manner, even sin itself works for them towards righteousness. "We know that for those who love God all things work together for good." Does not a fall work for us for good if we become humbler and more careful because of it?[79]

Even our sins can have an important role to play in our spiritual development. Failure breaks open the husk of self-confidence and summons us into the sphere of ultimate dependence on God. As Dorotheos of Gaza remarked: "The wretchedness of disobedience will teach you the rest of obedience as it says in the prophet (Jeremiah 2:19), 'Your apostasy will be your teacher.'"[80] The shock of sin can be a means by which we come to the realization of the unconditional character of God's love. As Francis Thomson wrote in *The Hound of Heaven*, "Who could love ignoble thee, save only me?" Listen now to Julian of Norwich.

For, in truth, we shall see in heaven for all eternity that though we have sinned grievously in this life, we were never hurt in God's love, nor were we ever of less value in God's sight. This falling is a test by which we shall have a high and marvelous knowing of love in God for ever. That love [of God] is hard and marvelous that cannot and will not be broken for our trespasses.[81]

In love mercy allows us to fail somewhat, and in failing we fall, and in falling we die. . . . Our failing is full of fear; our falling is marked by sin; our dying is sorrowful. Yet in all this the sweet eye of pity never departs from us and the working of mercy never ceases.[82]

At the same time, we need to be aware of the danger of blunting our consciences and coming to regard our failures too lightly. Joachim Jeremias writing on the Pharisees affirms that a loss of the sense of sin in religious persons has two main sources. The first is a casuistry that views sins in isolation and tries to negate guilt through clever distinctions, a system of distinguishing big and small sins so that small sins do not matter much so long as big sins are avoided. The second is a doctrine of merit whereby sins are counterbalanced with good deeds that are regarded as meritorious: "The only important thing is that in the final judgment merits should outweigh transgressions."[83]

All of this involves reducing sin to an external action. It ceases to see sin in terms of our personal relationship with God, and it becomes simply the violation of some legal requirement with the consequence that we have to pay the penalty. The malice of sin is more in the heart than in the action, and even a good action can be contaminated by a bad intention. As Thomas Becket says in T. S. Eliot's *Murder in the Cathedral*, "The last temptation was the greatest treason, / to do the right deed for the wrong reason." What we see in the sinful act is only the flower—we have also to consider the roots from which it springs. Long before a crime has been committed there has been a mental betrayal. It is this moment when the will gives its assent that sin is committed, not when the action itself is performed. I sin when I pull the trigger on the gun, even though, unknown to me, it is firing blanks. In Henry Purcell's opera *Dido and Aeneas*, Dido sings to Aeneas: "O feckless man . . . it is enough whate'er you now decree, that you had once thought of leaving me." Malice is as much expressed in the thought as in the commission of the act. This is why, as Jesus reminded us, the adulterous thought is equivalent to the act of adultery. Adultery can be committed not in fact but in the heart. We may be surprised that someone as innocent as Saint Therese of Lisieux did not see much difference between herself and a murderer who was about to be executed. She understood well to what depths the human heart may sink. It is probably true for most of us that to the extent that we are innocent of particular crimes it is most likely through lack of opportunity. We may be too timid to do the horrendous things our imagination sometimes conjures up, but this does not mean that we are not defiled by the mere imagining. This is why the ancient monks were adamant that we strictly monitor our thoughts.

Saint Aelred of Rievaulx, although he is very compassionate toward human weakness, insists that we must try to do something about the bad habits that are destroying the integrity of our lives, whether these be external actions or persistent patterns of thought. Interestingly enough he does not advise the moralists' cure-all and call on us to exert more will power, and to try harder. He takes a more tactical approach. Beginning at the cognitive level we need to demolish the rationalizations that support bad habits and to use ordinary means of containing and repairing the damage done. He proposes what we might call a five-point plan.[84]

1. We need first of all actively to detest the vice and to call it by its name instead of hiding behind denial and rationalization. In the words of Karl Barth, "we must call lies 'lies,' and abominations 'abominations.'" Saint Bernard notes that often we attempt to neutralize our consciences by giving new names to the vices we are too ashamed to acknowledge. We must desist from the practice of rebaptizing vices as if by giving them a nice name we can change their moral character. Gluttony is gluttony, it is not enjoying God's gifts. Avarice is avarice, it is not being prudent for the future. Lust is lust, it is not merely being natural and human. Fancy names and imaginative rationalizations change nothing; they merely lead us deeper into denial and delusion.

2.   He recommends that we accuse ourselves honestly, at least in the privacy of our conscience. We have to take full responsibility not only for actions but also, more especially, for omissions, since these are too easily overlooked. We also have to recognize our complicity in the accumulated momentum toward evil that followed the choices we have made and is expressed in the bad habits of thought, speech, and action that lead us to sin.

3.   He advises us to act as our own prosecutors and to make a case against the vice, to think through our situation honestly and try to construct a reasoned argument for improvement. For example, in a particular situation a person may engage in self-confrontation saying: "If you continue to drive under the influence of alcohol you may well be caught and end up in prison, you may hurt or kill another person or yourself, you may bring grief to your family, you may lose your employment, you may damage yourself financially." Not the noblest reasons but real possibilities. To the extent that persons still have control over their lives, such reflections will certainly slow down the destructive process and maybe reverse it. This suggestion is not unlike cognitive behavioral therapy.

4.   Saint Aelred advises us to listen to the reproaches of others. This includes those nearest and dearest to us, although sometimes it is our enemies who are the most eloquent and truthful in pointing out where we are going wrong. Instead of resenting it when others express their dissatisfaction with our performance, perhaps we should pay attention. If our failures are real, it would be a tragedy if we were the last to recognize what is happening. This is hard, but we need to develop tactics whereby we can take negative feedback to heart, seeing it as a possible message from God, intended not to hurt or humiliate us but to show us the error of our ways in the hope that we will amend.

5. Finally, he suggests that we ask God to extinguish the vice, and that we come before God in all simplicity, recognizing our impotence and our need for grace. In our helplessness we are impelled to cast ourselves on the mercy of God. We will find that God is responsive to this prayer—though not always in the manner for which we had hoped. "Those who sense that they are infested either by the promptings of nature or the suggestions of demons or by their own thoughts should send up the vehement wailing of their heart and the wretched lament of their voice with tears and sighs to God."[85]

The self-knowledge that comes from temptation is useless if it paralyzes us, like a rabbit caught in the brilliance of headlights. Self-knowledge is meant to serve as an incentive to get busy on several fronts to see whether, with the help of God, something may be done to improve the situation. We are called to vigilance, and this involves proactive and preemptive defense against potential temptation. Undoubtedly this is quite a heavy burden, but such vigilance is the means par excellence of making progress toward a more abundant life.

Lord Jesus Christ,

You taught us to desire an undivided heart.

Help us to recognize our ambiguities and compromises

And to leave aside whatever in our life is an obstacle to love

So that love may be our guide in all we say and do.

For you are our Lord, for ever and ever.

Amen!

CHAPTER SIX

The Grace of
Self-Knowledge

I mplicit in much of what we have been saying has been the
theme of self-knowledge. I do not consider it an exaggera-
tion to affirm that the gaining of self-knowledge is the most
important asceticism for all who aspire to live a spiritual life, as
well as the most enduring and the most laborious. It is also the
most paradoxical. It is a bit like the Heisenberg principle, which
says something to the effect that the act of observing and the consequent state of being observed change the situation that is under
observation. If we are aware that we are being watched by CCTV
cameras it is unlikely that we will act naturally. We will put on a
good show for the cameras. So it is with trying to see ourselves as
object. All we have to look at is what is on the surface—what we
ourselves consciously decide to make visible. We cannot see what
is underneath because what is visible is hiding it. So, increasing
the visibility of the observable self occludes the real self. The real
self is known as a subject; I know myself by being myself and by
expressing my authentic nature by faithful action, not by looking
at myself in some kind of mirror. The self cannot be known as an
object. It can, perhaps, be known intersubjectively, that is to say,
known in relationship, but even this knowledge is not immune
from surprises, and people will often be forced to say regretfully,
"I thought I knew that person!" If our subjective self-knowledge
were perfect, self-consciousness would disappear—not because
the self would no longer exist but because it had become perfectly

transparent. Its purest function is to be like a window so that the light of the spiritual world might radiate through it without let or hindrance. What we can see is mostly only camouflage.

That is probably enough metaphysics for now, so let me backtrack and pace out the idea in more familiar territory. I have already alluded to the importance of the distinction between the "true self" and the "false self" in the thought of Thomas Merton. Let me meander around this topic for a while.

When asked what he thought was the most significant problem facing the world today, the former General of the Jesuits Father Adolfo Nicolás replied, "the globalization of superficiality."[86] As we have already noted, by choosing to spend a great deal of our time entertaining ourselves, gawking at celebrities, and whiling away the hours in idle pursuits, we progressively lose our capacity to engage with anything at a profound level. You only have to look at the range of celebrity magazines, the space devoted to trivialities in what used to be quality newspapers, or the inanities of social media to be convinced that people—and I suppose this must include ourselves—are losing interest in thinking about serious topics. As a result, when it comes to self-assessment we will probably base our judgments on what we can know without too much trouble: our biographical history, our personality and attitudes, what others say about us, and other components of the knowable self that are—if you will excuse the oxymoron—profoundly superficial.

This is how Merton describes what we discover when our search to understand ourselves is limited to what is less significant.

> The self which we observe as it goes about its biological business, the machine which we regulate and tune up and feed with all kinds of stimulants and sedatives, constantly trying to make it run more smoothly, to fit the patterns prescribed by the salesmen of pleasure-giving and anxiety-allaying commodities.[87]

What we see of ourselves is mostly the effect of social conditioning—the roles and expectations assigned by others, on the one
hand, and, on the other, the disguises and masks we preemptively
assume in order to win approval and reward. To some extent,
coming to a fuller personal maturity is a process of diluting the
social conditioning to which we have been exposed—irrespective
of whether we consider the effects of such "formation" to have
been positive or negative. This implies a role for creative solitude
in which we can suspend our lifelong occupation of pleasing others and turn down the nagging voice of the superego and attempt
the Herculean task of just being ourselves, who we are, what we
are, where we have been, and where we are heading. When we are
alone we can discard the fig leaves and feel no shame. We are what
we are. Paradoxically, however, that is why many people are afraid
of solitude—they fear that without the masks and trappings behind
which they hide there is nothing worthwhile.

Self-acceptance involves, first of all, accepting the deep-down
duality of our lives. It means that we need to get behind the public
self to find out who we really are. Especially, it involves cutting
down on the spin we use to present ourselves to others in a favor-
able light. Perhaps the hardest part of embracing the hidden self
is to include in our acceptance those tendencies and feelings that
run counter to the demands and expectations not only of the
ego but also of the superego. Until we include these shadows in
our understanding of the self, our self-image will be partial and
distorted. The shadows we see are the direct result of a light shin-
ing. Shadows are abundant at noon; at midnight, there are none.
When we become more aware of the shadows in our life this is not
a retrograde moment, but an advance. A light shines and we see
reality more clearly. As Merton writes:

> The basic and fundamental problem of the spiritual life is
> the acceptance of our hidden and dark self, with which we

tend to identify all the evil that is in us. We must learn by discernment to separate the evil growth of our actions from the good ground of our soul. And we must prepare that ground so that a new life can spring us from it within us beyond our knowledge and beyond our conscious control.[88]

Until we have identified the shadows and found ways to prevent their secret influence on the choices by which we shape our lives, we cannot even begin to ponder ways of liberating our spiritual energies to do their transforming work within us. Our consciously chosen efforts to pursue a spiritual life will be constantly stymied by a fifth column of which we are unaware. The efforts we invest will not yield proportionate fruits. The harder we try the more we will seem bogged in the mud. No wonder we so easily become discouraged!

We cannot eliminate the negative polarity, but we can shine light upon its workings. And then we can try to bring about some degree of interior harmony. The more we are interiorly distressed at the way we are—and sometimes we should be!—the more we are motivated to do the things that lead to peace. Listen to Merton again.

The first thing you have to do, before you start thinking about such a thing as contemplation, is to try to recover your basic natural unity, to reintegrate your compartmentalized being into a coordinated and simple whole, and learn to live as a unified human person. This means that you have to bring back together the fragments of your distracted existence so that when you say "I" there is really someone present to support the pronoun you have uttered.[89]

The key to the process is truth. Just as the life of Jesus in Nazareth was ordinary, obscure, and laborious, so our own lives do not have to be so glamorous. We are not celebrities, but our greatest hope is to be numbered among God's faithful people—the "little ones" for whom the kingdom is reserved. So, the true self is often humbler and more humdrum than the false self; it is what it is and doesn't have to dress itself up to look better. And usually the real self is better humored, less temperamental, and less liable to throw tantrums or sulk.

> The inner self is not an *ideal* self, especially not an imaginary, perfect creature fabricated to measure up to our compulsive need for greatness, heroism and infallibility. On the contrary, the real "I" is just simply ourself and nothing more. Nothing more, nothing less. Our self as we are in the eyes of God, to use Christian terms. Our self in all our uniqueness, dignity, littleness and ineffable greatness. . . . [Our] real and "homely" self, and nothing more, without glory, without self-aggrandizement, without self-righteousness and without self-concern.[90]

This secret self with its still, small voice is the only one capable of entering into an authentic relationship with God, "who resists the proud and gives grace to the humble." As Merton reminded us in a text already quoted:

> Unless we discover this deep self, which is hidden with Christ in God, we will never really know ourselves as persons. Nor will we know God. For it is by the doors of this deep self that we enter into the spiritual knowledge of God.[91]

Not to find the true self means remaining at the level of the superficial self and growth toward the fullness of the authentic self is truncated. We become like actors who play particular roles and in the public mind are identified with the characters they portray. And sometimes it happens that they begin to see themselves as the embodiments of their fictional roles. Gary Burghoff, who played Radar in *M.A.S.H.*, was annoyed that even his mother called him "Radar." An actor who played a nun in the Australian series *Brides of Christ* was occasionally interviewed as some sort of expert on religious life. In the same way, we often think that the role or roles we play to please others constitute the only reality we have. Merton sees this role-playing not only as the end of any hope of real spiritual growth but also as an expression of sinfulness. As long as we remain alienated from who and what we are, we are also alienated from God. It is only by operating at the level of the true self that we are able to form community. The cohabitation of false selves, when many phonies attempt to live together, is an invitation to pantomime authentic community; on the surface, everything may look good to observers, but underneath it is purgatory.

All sin starts from the assumption that my false self, the self that exists only in my egocentric desires, is the fundamental reality of life to which everything else in the universe is ordered. Thus I use up my life in the desire for pleasures and the thirst for experiences, for power, honor, knowledge and love, to clothe this false self and construct its nothingness into something objectively real. And I wind experiences round myself and cover myself with pleasures and glory like bandages in order to make myself perceptible to myself and to the world, as if I were an invisible body that could only become visible when something visible covered its surface. But there is no substance under the things with which I am clothed. I am hollow, and the structure of pleasures and ambitions has no foundation. I am objectified in them. But they are all destined by their very contingency to be destroyed. And when they are gone there will be nothing

left of me but my own nakedness and emptiness and hol-
lowness, to tell me that I am my own mistake.[92]

Merton may have been thinking of the 1937 film *The Invisible
Man*, based on the novel by H. G. Wells and the poignancy of not
being able to be seen by others. At first glance there seemed to be
obvious advantages to being invisible, but it is an ultimately lonely
existence.

At this point Merton evokes the paschal mystery. The gospel
teaches that the only way to gain one's life is to lose it.

> In order to become oneself, one must die. That is to say, in
> order to become one's true self, the false self must die. . . .
> [This involves] a deepening of the new life, a continuous
> rebirth, in which the exterior and superficial life of the ego-
> self is discarded like an old snakeskin and the mysterious,
> invisible self of the Spirit becomes more present and more
> active.[93]

If I have devoted a good deal of space in this chapter to
Merton's thought, it is because it is important and is expressed in
a language that is more familiar to us. As is often the case, Merton
is expressing fairly traditional teaching in more contemporary
language. We will find similar conclusions being drawn in the
Western ideas about self-will, *propria voluntas*. The problem with
self-will is not only that it strives to live without interference from
others, including God, but also that in doing so it cuts itself from
any possibility of discovering one's own giftedness and receiving
encouragement from others to pursue paths of greater creativity.
As Saint Benedict's description of the false monks in RB 1.6-9
indicates, self-will is a matter of maintaining full control over
one's own life and living it for one's own advantage, convenience,
and gratification. *Proprietas* is opposed to *communitas*; self-will

torpedoes any hope of genuine community. Perhaps we would employ the terms *selfishness* or *individualism*, but these terms are too mild to describe the reality for which the Latin word *singularitas* was used. Self-will implies that we ourselves are the only ones taken into consideration in the making of choices; nobody else matters. As the thirteenth-century Cistercian Baldwin of Forde wrote: "If someone lives only for himself and for his own advantage, and considers only himself in deciding how he should live, we can understand [this whole life] to be wholly dark."[94] It has to be said that among all the challenges we face, the principal demand of gospel living in whatever form, including monastic life, is the renunciation of self-will. As Aelred of Rievaulx notes, "The perfection of monks consists in setting aside self-will."[95]

Actions that are the consequence of self-will are both the cause and effect of alienation from the community expressed in marginalization, passive aggression, the blocking of initiatives, all of which lead to stalemate, and sometimes open hostility.[96] Just as doing things together builds up a sense of community, so deliberately doing things differently and, as a result, progressively developing a self-chosen and distinctive identity can be more than an expression of my own sense of alienation. It can also serve as a symbolic slap in the face to everyone else.

> I say that [an act of] self-will is one that is not shared with God or with other persons. It is ours alone. It is when what we will we do for our own sake, not for the honor of God or for the service of the brethren, not intending to please God or to be of profit to the brethren to satisfy our own interior tendencies.[97]

There is an abundance of monastic literature on self-will; in Merton's terms this is living according to the false self. Bernard goes a step farther. More serious than self-will and often its cause is what he terms "self-counsel," *proprium consilium*. This means having my own views on everything, insulated from what others hold. Note that what is being referred to is closer to "opinion" than to "knowledge" and, of course, is far away from "science." It means simply that I have my own way of looking at things, my own system of values, my own "principles," my own standards, by which I judge what is important and what is not.

> [*Proprium consilium*] is what belongs to those who have a zeal for God but not according to knowledge. They pursue their own error and are stubborn in it so that they do not want to agree with any advice that is given them. They cause division where there was unity, they are the enemies of peace, they lack charity, they are swollen with vanity, pleasing themselves and being great in their own eyes, ignorant of the righteousness of God and wanting to set up their own [in its place]. What greater pride is there when one person prefers his own judgment to that of the whole community as if he alone had the Spirit of God?[98]

There is something similar in Ephesians 2:3. Speaking about of preconversion life, the author notes in the middle of a long sentence, "We were living then in the desires of our flesh and doing the things willed by the flesh and by the mind." The word used here, *dianoia*, is the Septuagint equivalent to *leb*, the heart as the seat of understanding, the mind as the organ of *noein*. If the mind is debased then not only are the actions it commends wrong, but they seem to the doer of them to be unquestionably right. In the manuals of moral theology this was termed "invincible error"—a wrong view that is resistant to reasoning. Persons who have lost the sense of taste not only are unable to distinguish between sweet and salty, but are also unaware that they lack this ability. It is a double liability.

Self-knowledge is the basis of our capacity to find our way through the forest of contrary imaginations and impulses through which our life passes. It enables us to begin a process of discernment (*diakrisis* or *discretio*) whether by introspection and self-examination or by seeking counsel from another. It is through effective self-knowledge that the effort we invest in the spiritual pursuit is most likely to produce proportionate fruit.

> Nothing is more effective and speedier in bringing a soul to humility than for it to discover the truth in its own regard. There is no scope here for dissimulation or deceit. On the contrary, the soul should simply confront itself without averting its gaze.[99]

The effects of self-knowledge are not only immanent, they are also transitive. This is just a fancy way of saying that we are not its only beneficiaries. When we live in truth those around us profit. A little bit of humility in our own regard takes away some of the sharp edges of our coexistence and often softens our judgments of others. As Aelred notes, losing sight of our own liabilities will lead us to pay more attention to the foibles and faults of others. It is not a slight matter; it undermines our union with Christ's faithful people.

> There is no doubt that those who take their eyes off themselves, being unwilling to pay attention to themselves, that is to their own weakness, but preferring to examine the lives of others and pass judgment on them, such people depart from their membership of Christ's flock and [instead] feed their own carnal senses with wicked and sinful delight.[100]

Self-Knowledge leads to a growth in empathy—an ability to feel compassion for those in trouble and to act from that feeling. It is easy enough, even in a good community, to be so involved in one's own life and its issues that we feel a certain indifference to the afflictions of others.[101]

Another quality of self-knowledge is that it helps us to appreciate that God's love is unconditional. When we remain at the level of truth all our assets appear as gifts. As one of the texts already quoted from Merton states, "It is by the doors of this deep self that we enter into the spiritual knowledge of God." In this context we may recall *The Cloud of Unknowing*, "Toil and sweat in all that you are able to acquire a true knowing and feeling of yourself, a wretch, as you are. Then, I believe, soon afterwards you will have a true knowing and feeling of God as he is . . . as he allows himself to be known and experienced by a meek soul living in this mortal body."[102] Self-knowledge leads to a celebration of the love of God, which is described in the first chapter of Ephesians, gratuitous, rich, and abundant.

In one of the longest sentences he wrote, comprising 104 words, Saint Bernard lists all the mishaps we can experience on our earthly pilgrimage and then dismisses their capacity to diminish God's love in our regard. There is nothing our sins can do to cause God to reverse the choice made in creating us. But first we have to be honest in our self-assessment.

It is my teaching that every soul although burdened with sins, although caught in the trap of vices, although captured by allurements, although a captive in exile, although imprisoned in its body, although clinging to the mud and stuck in the mire, although bound to its bodily members, although pierced through by worries, pulled apart by business, contracted by fears, afflicted with sorrows, led astray by errors, made anxious by responsibilities, and unsettled by suspicions, although it is a traveler in a hostile country and thus, as the Prophet says, soiled by contact with the dead and reckoned with those in hell. . . .

At this point most readers will have identified with at least one of the conditions that Bernard lists with so much eloquence. Then he continues his sentence, insisting that none of these miseries has any capacity to block God's plans for us.

> . . . this is what I say that although a soul is so condemned and so desperate, nevertheless it is my teaching that such a soul is able to find within itself not only a source of relief in the hope of pardon so that it may hopefully seek mercy, but also it will find a source of boldness that it may desire marriage with the Word, not fearing to enter into a treaty of friendship with God, nor being timid about taking up the yoke of love from him who is the King of Angels . . .

Forgiveness of sins is too little to expect from God's mercy; we may also boldly and legitimately desire the closest union with God, in this life and the next. The basis for this claim is not that we have merited such favor, but simply that it is the realization of God's plan for us when we were created in his image and likeness.

> For what cannot be safely dared when the soul sees itself as his excellent image and distinguished likeness?[103]

We may have made a mess of our lives according to our own estimation and, perhaps, that of others, but nothing has changed in the way that God regards us. Such goals as self-actualization, contemplation, transparency, purity of heart, and the like are not beyond us. The God who wills that all are to be saved has gladly included us in that number. If we understood more fully the boundless love with which God has brought us into being and the power God has to bring good even out of evil, then we would be always bouncing with joy and hope and fired up with a confidence that God will indeed bring to completion the good work that has been begun.

Loving Father,
You have created us in your own image
So that we might come to know you and love you.
Help us to live in the truth of what you have designed us
*   to be,*
Casting away all falsehood and delusion
And living in the freedom that belongs to your children.
We make this prayer in the name of Jesus, our Lord.
Amen!

CHAPTER SEVEN

The Grace of Prayer: Petition

One of my favorite aphorisms about prayer is from Saint Augustine: "Because I am human, therefore I am weak. Because I am weak, therefore I pray."[104] One of the fruits of self-knowledge is an increased dependence on the grace of God. When we have (finally) become convinced of the precariousness of our virtue and the ease with which we could fall away, our faith generates in us a heartfelt appeal to God for help that extends itself over our past, our present, and our future. We pray for forgiveness and healing; we pray for guidance and courage; we pray for ongoing support and the precious gift of perseverance. Although our prayer is generated by our own neediness, progressively it reaches out to include in its embrace the whole of creation. In a sense, all prayer is directed to the coming of God's kingdom. From our acutely felt personal needs prayer expands to become the voice of all humanity. In his instruction to an anchoress, Saint Aelred tells her to embrace the whole world with the arms of her prayer. Progressively our prayer will follow the same course.

In a single act of love hold the entire world in your heart. There consider all the good people together and rejoice. There look upon the evil and lament. Gaze upon those in trouble and oppressed and share their suffering. Within your soul encounter the wretchedness of the poor, the wailing of orphans, the desolation of widows, the grief of those who mourn, the troubles of travelers, the dangers of those at sea, the offerings of virgins, the temptations of monks, the cares of prelates, the labor of soldiers. Open to all the breast of your love. Let your tears flow for them. Pour out your prayers for them.[105]

In one of his precious statements about prayer, Jesus makes the surprising recommendation that we should make our requests to God without discernment, not making a judgment (Mk. 11:23). So surprising that, even though we find the same admonition in the Epistle of James, (Jas. 1:6), it is usually not adequately translated. The text of Mark reads: "Amen I say to you that if anyone says to this mountain, 'Be lifted up and cast into the sea,' and does not judge in his heart but believes that what he says will happen, so it will be for him." Usually the verb *diakrinein* is translated in these texts as "hesitate" or "doubt." There could be several causes of hesitation or doubt, but in this case the reluctance to believe comes from spending too much time weighing up the possibilities before committing oneself to make a request. Instead of saying out our request to God we attempt to filter our prayer before sending it, making sure the content is respectable and the manner of expression appropriate. Just as we would with an earthly superior. Prayer is the interaction of faith and our real situation. We have to let it flow. We may not allow a censor to block it or convert it into something different. We do not have to make our prayer respectable; it is an intimate interchange between God and ourselves—it is not going to be published or disseminated on the Internet. It has to be real. To pray well we need the Spirit's gift of boldness, *parrhesia*—a real freedom to say things as they are; there is no need to dissemble.

Many people seem to confuse God with Queen Victoria of England. Of Queen Victoria it is known that not only was she the ruler of an empire on which the sun never set, but she was also the mother of a large family. Her maternal role was held up to the mothers of the empire for their admiration and imitation. As far as her royal duties allowed, she would spend time with her children, holding the babies, playing with the infants, and asking the older ones what they had learned in school. What she didn't know, but we do, is that for the children the whole day revolved around this hour spent with their mother. They all arrived rested and washed and fed. The older ones were rehearsed in the answers they had to give about the day's new learnings. No doubt Her Majesty was gratified to see how content and polite and dutiful her children were, and it was a pleasant time for all. But this is scarcely what motherhood is about. Real mothers have to deal with children who are tired and cranky, sick or anxious, disobedient and sulky. The nature of maternal love is shown in how mothers respond to these negativities without rejecting their children or withholding their love. A real mother's love is exceedingly robust; it can cope with anything. This is an infinitely better picture of God's love than the regal maternity of Queen Victoria. When Jesus presents God as Father, he means that we do not have to dress up to present ourselves or to pretend to be what we are not. Fathers and mothers accept their children as they are and continue to love them whatever they do.

Jesus was at pains to remind us often of the Father's universal and unconditional love. "God causes the sun to rise on the evil and the good, and sends rain on the righteous and the unrighteous" (Matt. 5:45). "God is kind to the ungrateful and wicked" (Lk. 6:35). We do not have to disguise our reality so as to appear before God as somehow better than we are. We do not have to turn our prayer into a well-rehearsed theatrical performance. It was for being playactors (the base meaning of the word translated as "hypocrisy") that Jesus criticized the Pharisees. We are to come before God just as we are—not so much because that is something wonderful, but because God's acceptance is all-embracing. No matter what we do we cannot relocate ourselves to a zone outside God's love. All too often our difficulties in prayer come simply from a notion of God that does not do justice to the robust vigor of divine mercy. We have already quoted the text in which Julian of Norwich wrote, "[God's] love is hard and marvelous, for it cannot and will not be broken for trespasses." Our personal history can never become an obstacle to our access to God. On the contrary, it is the springboard from which the desire of our hearts leaps beyond self to the infinity of the spiritual world.

Authentic prayer grows out of authentic living. At some stage in our life we have to make the transition from being "good" to being ourselves. It is only when we have passed this midpoint (at whatever chronological age it occurs) that a life-changing prayer slowly grows within us—although, as Mark's Gospel reminds us, it will not necessarily be without persecutions. When we are cocooned within the roles and expectations others impose on us we feel a certain sense of security and, as a result, prayer is often perfunctory; it is part of the dull routine by which we are expected to live. It is only when we risk walking on the sea that we learn to cry out with the utmost sincerity, "Save me, Lord, I am perishing."

I suppose it is worth asking ourselves how smooth we expect our spiritual journey to be. How upset do we get when we encounter a few bumps on the road or worse? In one sense, you might say that the difficulties we encounter are there precisely to serve as a reminder of reality and to give us a nudge to turn back to prayer. In his commentary on the Fourth Gospel, Rudolf Bultmann speaks of revelation as crisis (*krisis*); the coming of Christ changed everything; it was no longer possible to sit on the fence. A decision for or against the revelation has to be made. Revelation creates division (schism), depending on people's willingness or not to accept it.[106] Turning this proposition inside out we might speak of crisis as revelation. When our familiar world tumbles into ruins, it is easier to see beyond its constraining walls. We may go further and say that whenever we find ourselves precipitated into a state of anxiety, confusion, misunderstanding, rejection, its hidden meaning is that we are being called to find Christ and thus to intensify our prayer. This may be easier said than done. In times of trouble it is even harder to go beyond our present disturbance and relocate, as it were, in a zone of peace and acceptance, but we need to try. And keep trying. Of course, on a practical level, we can take steps to identify cause and to soften effects, but if we are wise we will use the opportunity to strengthen the bonds that unite us to Christ and through Christ to God. All things work together unto good for those who love God, even our mistakes and tragedies.

Choosing life, as Deuteronomy repeatedly admonishes, involves a global self-acceptance that teaches us to stand naked before the all-seeing eye of God, before whom everything is open and nothing is concealed, who sees what is hidden from mortal gaze. We are to throw away the fig leaves gathered by Adam and Eve and learn to be fearless and unashamed. In the presence of our all-loving and all-accepting Father, our proper self-love (*autophilia*) and our self-acceptance are strengthened and confirmed. This leads us to accept ourselves with all our liabilities, our inconsistencies, our failures—the mess that may well constitute the nonpublic side of our lives. We may not reject what God accepts.

In the early 1960s Canon Maurice Nédoncelle undertook a phenomenological study of prayer, published in English in 1964 with the rather uninspiring title *The Nature and Use of Prayer*.[107] He came to the conclusion that all prayer, including the highest moments of contemplative ecstasy, is at least implicitly petitionary. It is expressive of the truth of our relationship with God, which is always a matter of giving and receiving: God gives and we receive. As Friedrich Schleiermacher concluded, all religion stems from the experience of absolute dependence. To strive for complete autonomy in which we do not have to depend on anyone else is not only delusional, it is also moving in the direction of Luciferian pride. We are dependent on God, and it is only right that we experience this need and this dependence at all times but, especially, at the time of prayer.

For our prayer to be truthful it needs to reflect our life, whether that life be worthy or in a bit of a mess. If our prayer stinks it is often because our life stinks. Look no further! So, if I go to prayer and I spend the time distracted, then move on to strong feelings of anger, resentment, or bitterness; that is expressive of the reality of my life and is an appropriate starting point for my prayer. We cannot begin our prayer from anywhere except from where we are. Whether we express an inability to deal with emotions that have been aroused in us or whether our thoughts are dominated by trivial, self-centered, and immature desires, it makes no sense to approach God while pretending that this is not the case. It is better to spend the time contentedly agonizing over our prayerlessness than to attempt to fill the space with substitute activity, rattling off words, engaging in introspection, or using our imagination or reason. Fake prayer, arrived at by the indiscriminate use of techniques, profits nothing. All it does is to insulate us from the reality of who and what we are. We go to God as we are. Standing before God in truth is the first step in arriving at some remedy for our inadequacy. "Even though our hearts condemn us, God is greater than our hearts" (1 John 3:20). God sees the whole narrative, not just a single episode. But note. Our present situation is meant to be a point of departure—something to which we advert before passing it over to God, not something that dominates the whole program of our prayer.

This connection of prayer with our reality is a point that is strongly emphasized in Saint John Cassian's ninth *Conference*, attributed to Abba Isaac.

Prayer is fashioned anew from moment to moment according to the measure in which the mind is purified and according to the sort of situation in which it finds itself, whether this be the result of external contingencies or its own doing. It is certain, moreover that nobody is ever able to keep praying in the same way. Persons pray in one manner when they are cheerful and in another when they are weighed down by sadness or a sense of hopelessness. When they are flourishing spiritually their prayer is different from when they are oppressed by the extent of their struggles. They pray in one way when they are seeking pardon for their sins and in another when they are asking for some grace or virtue or for the elimination of a particular vice. Sometimes prayer is conditioned by compunction, occasioned by the thought of hell and the fear of judgment; at other times it is aflame with hope and desire for the good things to come. Persons pray in one manner when they find themselves in dangerous straits and in another when they enjoy quiet and security. Prayer is sometimes illumined by the revelation of heavenly mysteries, but at other times one is forced to be content with the sterile practice of virtue and the experience of aridity.[108]

The conclusion is "that there are as many forms of prayer as there are states of soul." There is always a prayer for this moment. The difficulties many of us experience often come from trying to recycle yesterday's prayer, paying no attention to the prayer of today.

Jesus was a man of prayer, and the teaching on prayer that we find in the Gospel tradition touches some of the most practical points that are likely to cause us some difficulty.

1. The parable about the Pharisee and the tax collector (Lk. 11:9–14) is an ongoing reminder that we are never too unworthy to pray and that it is more likely that our good deeds will block our prayer than the actions that make us uncomfortable. If you want to pray well beware of virtue— at least beware of seeming virtuous in your own eyes.

2. The parable about the unjust judge (Lk. 18:1–8) begins with the exhortation that we should keep on praying and not lose heart but keep on knocking, seeking, asking, even when it seems improbable that our prayer will make an impact.

3. Jesus's teaching about mountain-removal (Mk. 11:23) is an invitation to pray even though our prayer does not seem to make any sense. Prayer for "the impossible" is probably the best prayer since it is based on acceptance of the affirmation that "With God nothing is impossible" (Mt. 19:26).

4. Jesus's own example in Gethsemane (Mk. 14:32–42) shows us that there is a place even for the kind of prayer that seems to go against God's plan for us. In Mark's narrative, especially, we see the transformative effect of prayer, even when it does not achieve its stated aims. At the beginning of the pericope Jesus is falling apart; at the end he has regained his self-possession and even his sense of irony. We are changed by dialogue with God. As we pray for a particular need sometimes the unseen side of the situation appears to us; we see things differently, and perhaps there is a shift in the content of our petition. Prayer works mainly by changing us.

5. Throughout the Gospel tradition we find encouragement to make known our needs to God and to have confidence that our prayer will always achieve a positive result— whether that corresponds with what we asked for is another question, but we should not dismiss the possibility too lightly. We may find that often even our simplest and most

banal prayers seem to have been heard—even though we do not know by what means the desired result was brought about.

Jesus does not tell us to expect God to accommodate himself to our whims and wishes and then to change the world on our account. What he tells us to do is to express in a frank and filial way whatever we wish to ask of him. The discourse at the Last Supper emphasizes this. Our job is to keep making our petitions. This is part of the mix by which God's providence works, even if it is only we who are changed and not the world.

Jesus's most important contribution to our prayer is giving us an example of the form it is to take: the Lord's Prayer is a truly precious gift. At some stage in our life we need to adopt this prayer as our own. This may involve looking at the text exegetically. More important is our being able to say the prayer as though it comes from deep inside us, wrestling with each phrase until we can identify with it. Sometimes we may be helped by expanding the clauses or paraphrasing them, expressing them in words that come more easily from the heart.

We should never be ashamed to pray for ourselves or for others, nor should we think that "real men don't pray." In his essay on self-reliance, Ralph Waldo Emerson wrote that prayers are a symptom of an unhealthy will.[109] On the contrary, time spent in prayer can be among the most healthy and truthful moments of our life. In particular, we should not abandon simple intercessory prayer for those dear to us, for members of our family or community, for our enemies. We should be mindful of Saint Benedict's recommendation regarding the marginalized (or excommunicated) in the community. "If [the abbot] sees that nothing results from his efforts let him bring into play what is greater, his own prayer and that of the brothers so that the Lord, who can do all things, may bring health to the sick brother" (RB 28.4–5).

We confidently make our petitions to God because this is how Jesus instructed us—both by word and example. We may begin our prayer by boldly speaking out our needs, but progressively such itemization becomes unnecessary. We feel that it is sufficient to stand naked before the all-seeing mercy of our Father. Soon what is evident to God becomes self-evident to us. It is sufficient for us to be in God's presence. Although our stance before God is implicitly petitionary, it is no longer necessary for us to speak out our requests. Our needs speak for themselves. We don't have to understand the mechanics of how prayer works. We are simply commanded to pray. And, so, we make our prayer in the name of Jesus, our Lord. We are honest and sincere in our prayers because we are empowered by the Holy Spirit so that we may dare to address God as Father. We make our prayer boldly because all things are possible for God and all things work together unto good for those who love God and come before him as his children.

Loving Father,
Your love for us is beyond measure
And your concern touches every aspect of our lives.
Give us a strong faith that
All things are possible to you
And that all that comes from your hand is good.
Keep us safe in the dangerous passages of life
And protect the gift that you have given us.
We ask this in the name of Jesus the Lord. Amen!

CHAPTER EIGHT

The Grace of Prayer: Dedication

In 1943 Eugene Boylan published his bestselling book on prayer, *Difficulties in Mental Prayer*. It was reissued in 2010, but by then the title had probably lost its punch.[110] In 1943 priests, seminarians, and religious inevitably experienced difficulties during the obligatory daily exercise of mental prayer, but by 2010, a cynic such as myself might say that such difficulties had largely disappeared. Not because the quality of prayer had miraculously improved, but simply because such sessions were no longer enforced and many of those who found the going too hard simply abandoned the attempt at "mental prayer" and went off to do something more useful.

In a community that lives according to a rule, and for those who create a rule of life for themselves, a substantial amount of time is already allocated to prayer, perhaps in the form of the liturgy, particularly the Liturgy of the Hours. And many of us remain faithful to the daily practice of lectio divina, though the proportion of that which can be properly termed prayer varies from one day to the next and from one person to another. I take this substantial investment in such activities as given. Here I want to concentrate on the challenge of private prayer. What I would like to do at this point is to sing the praises of prayer as drudgery, and to affirm that one of the most important components of our approach to prayer is doggedness. I take this word from one of the letters of Flannery O'Connor, published in *The Habit of*

Being. "The only force I believe in is prayer, and it is a force I apply with more doggedness than attention."[111] In the beginning, most of us would have been aghast at such a statement, but as the years pass, we know from experience how challenging it is to maintain our practice of daily prayer and regularly to allocate to it a solid chunk of time.

"Nothing is so precious as time." So speaks the author of *The Cloud of Unknowing* (chapter 4)—even in the fourteenth century.[112] When I voluntarily make time for prayer I am giving to God what is most precious. I could be reading, I could be resting, I could be relaxing, I could be relating—but I have withdrawn from these desirable and life-enhancing activities to be in the presence of God. There are so many good works in which I could be employed. Although this is true, perhaps I need to remind myself that there is no end to possible employments and, perhaps, I need to learn to give a higher priority to what is truly important and of long-term significance over what is ephemeral and merely urgent.

I think we do a disservice to the importance of personal prayer when we fail to mention the challenge it poses, especially as life gets busier and the various activities that consume the minutes and the hours multiply unnoticed. The only way for prayer to have a significant role in our lives is for us to take a stand and insist on it. This means that self-giving or dedication is an essential component of prayer. Prayer is a means by which we offer ourselves and what is most precious to God. What we did when we committed ourselves to living a spiritual life or in coming to a monastery we continue to do when we clear space in our lives for the practice of prayer. Again, here is Canon Nédoncelle speaking about the very nature of prayer, whether it is prayer to God or to another human person.

Every prayer contains an offering and even a sacrifice. We inconvenience ourselves, we give up something, and what we give up we offer to the other person. It is the impulse to offer oneself that really matters; the movement begins from within. When this inner movement is made manifest by the yielding up of some material possession, the renunciation becomes symbolical, and therefore the manner of giving is more important than the gift itself.[113]

In this context, it is the allocation of time that matters, not what happens or does not happen during that period. It is what we put into prayer, not what we take out of it that matters. What happens is beyond our manipulation. "Your prayer will show what condition you are in. Theologians say that prayer is the monk's mirror," said Saint John Climacus.[114] We are what we are in prayer: there is no success or failure—just as what we see in the mirror is what we are. If we do not like what we see, there is no point in throwing out the mirror. That changes nothing. If we do not like the self we discover when we try to pray, the solution is not to stop praying. What we have to do is to turn our dissatisfaction into prayer so that in time things may change a little.

Meanwhile it is important that we continue to offer ourselves to God—in whatever state we are. Here we have some good models. Remember this poignant incident recounted in the Gospel of Mark.

And sitting opposite the collection boxes [Jesus] saw how the crowd was throwing copper coins into the boxes. And many rich people threw in much. Then came one poor widow who threw in two coins worth less than a penny. And calling his disciples to him [Jesus] said to them, "Amen I say to you that this widow, poor as she is, has thrown in more than all those who have thrown [money] into the collection boxes. For all of them threw in what was superfluous, but she, in her neediness, threw in all that she had, her whole living." (Mk. 12:41–44)

This is a potent lesson in changing the way we evaluate actions. Quantitative judgments miss the point; it is what comes out from the heart that endows the gift with value. The widow's offering was special because she gave her all. None of the rich contributors could match that. In a similar way, we may well feel that our prayer is not much to write home about, but it costs us and it is the best we can do. While other believers seem to be ecstatic about their practice of prayer, we are scrabbling around in the mud. There is no need for us to feel envious. It may well be that mud-prayer is more truthful in our case and that the work it is doing in our lives is more potent and more significant.[115] Prayer is actively truthful; it cannot be tricked. And whatever we may feel or think about its quality it necessarily accomplishes something good in us. We may feel ashamed at the thought that others might find out how muddy our prayer is, but that is the best we can do—the two small coins that seem worthless to the elite but are deemed precious by God.

We can, if we please, find another image of generous giving in Mark's narrative of the woman who anointed Jesus's feet with expensive ointment.

While [Jesus] was in Bethany, reclining [at the table] in the house of Simon the Leper, a woman came with an alabaster jar of very expensive ointment of pure nard. She broke the alabaster and poured the ointment on his head. Some of those present were angry [saying] to one another, "Why this waste of ointment? This ointment could have been sold for more than three hundred denarii and given to the poor." And they rebuked her. But Jesus said, "Leave her alone. Why do you give her a hard time? She has done a beautiful act to me. The poor you will always have with you; you can do good to them any time you wish. But me you will not always have. She did what she could. Before the time she anointed my body for burial. Amen, I say to you, wherever in the whole world the Good News is proclaimed, what she has done will also be spoken of, in memory of her." (Mk. 14:3–9)

Here again is an image of extravagant giving that flies in the face of functional rationality: A gift that defies utility. A beautiful and gratuitous gesture. But it is also an act of prophecy—it has a deeper meaning. It somehow typifies the wasteful expenditure of Christ's life that will have an impact on the whole world. A gift given to God is never lost; it remains forever.

Time given to prayer is bread cast upon the waters of eternity. It is not lost. To those who have effectively given up the practice of regular private prayer because they are "not getting anything out of it" I usually say, "Who says you have to get anything out of it. It is far more important that you put something into it." Prayer is an act of self-giving: we give our time. We suspend the useful activities in which we are engaged. We redirect our attention away from what interests us. We move away from the visible and tangible and stretch out toward the invisible. Our exercise of prayer is defined by the alternatives of which we let go. We cannot produce prayer—that is the work of the Holy Spirit; all we can do is reduce other occupations.

This is what we find exemplified in the life of Jesus as portrayed in the Gospels. Although he was God's Son, as he went around doing good he understood the necessity of setting aside space and time for intimate communion with his Father in a way that was not possible during the activities of an ordinary day. Let us look at one example from the Gospel of Mark, coming from the earliest phase of Jesus's public ministry. "And rising at morning while it was still very dark, [Jesus] went out and went away to a deserted place and there he prayed" (Mk. 1:35). Thus, in a single verse, Jesus's practice of prayer is portrayed. It is a very dense sentence, and each part of it calls out to be considered carefully.

1. *Rising*

Prayer is a resurrection. Whether it is getting up after a night's sleep or becoming more mindful after a spate of absorbing activities, all prayer represents a change at the level of consciousness. As Augustine often avers, God is present in our lives, but we are not present to God. Although, by baptism, we were established in a filial relationship with God—in a state of prayer—most of the time we live in a fog of forgetfulness. At the level of being we are one with God, but at the level of consciousness we are far distant. Our effort at prayer is the struggle to become aware of the grace in which we live, to transform mindlessness into mindfulness, to bring an end to our forgetfulness of God and allow God to speak to our hearts. In prayer we take time to remember God, to be mindful of God, to break out from our confinement in space and time and to reach out to eternity. Prayer is a time in which we reorient our lives toward God, we rise up from confusion and slackness, cast off the paralysis of procrastination, and make a positive choice to allow God entry into our hearts and our lives. No longer spiritually dead or half dead, we are on the move toward God and toward a more abundant life. As we were addressed at baptism, so we are summoned to prayer. "Rise up, O Sleeper, arise from among the dead and Christ will shine upon you" (Eph. 5:14). "Arise and shine for your light has come" (Isa. 60:1). "I shall be filled, when I awake, with the sight of your glory" (Ps. 17:15). At the time of prayer, we are called to live differently from other times—to be aware of aspects of reality that at other times escape our notice.

2. *at morning*

Getting up early usually requires planning—especially in a period of history when roosters were the only alarm clocks. What Jesus did was a calculated act. Prayer is too important to be left to accident. For many of us the opportunity to spend a substantial time in prayer depends on our willingness to adopt a rule of life in which prayer is built into our daily routine. Since, in most places, there are only twenty four hours in a day, this will mean that some of the other activities by which the hours are filled will have to be abbreviated or left aside. We may have to curtail our sleep. We may need to review the time we spend on social media and entertainment. We may need to bring our workload back into reasonable limits. We cannot hope to deepen our life of union with God unless prayer increases, first in quantity and then, almost inevitably, in quality. We have to stop hoping to *find* time for prayer; there is no time to be found. We have to begin to *make* time for prayer, and this will always be at the expense of alternative pursuits.

Western culture cherishes spontaneity and, as a result, tends to underestimate the importance of routine in attaining goals. A little reflection on our experience shows that spontaneity is much overvalued in terms of achieving goals. The only way for an exercise program to achieve its desired results is for it to be embraced regularly and perseveringly. The only way for an artist, musician, or writer to become good at their work is to keep at their regular routines even when initial enthusiasm has waned and practice has become a chore. It is the same with prayer. Sometimes, especially at the beginning, spending time with God is delightful. Paradoxically, as we advance in the spiritual life, prayer often becomes drier and less appealing. We are inclined to find alternative activities that permit us to abandon, abbreviate, or defer the solitary time spent in personal prayer. Usually this is not a deliberate choice we make that will bind us for the rest of our life. More often it is an option only for today, when there is more work, when the weather is unpleasant, when I am not in the mood, when there is something enjoyable to do. But then, the same situation recurs tomorrow, and before I know it, personal prayer has begun to slide out of my usual life and it becomes an exception rather than the rule.

We must build into our usual daily schedule time spent with God. Even if it is only the practice recommended in the *Didache* of reciting the Lord's Prayer morning, noon, and night, that is better than leaving everything to chance. If we are serious in our commitment to God we need to shore up that commitment with regular prayer. This is not to say that there will never be exceptions or relaxations, but it is a matter of setting up some structures that ensure that we stay in touch and do not become strangers to God.

3. *while it was still very dark*

The early hours of the day have a special claim on our attention when we are considering a time for prayer. They come before everything else begins to happen. To schedule the main bulk of our prayer first thing in the morning means that we give priority to prayer. In practice, of course, this means scheduling our time for going to bed so that we get enough sleep. It is much more difficult to pray if we are sleep-deprived, as so many are today. Cardinal Newman once wrote, "Go to bed on time, and you are already perfect."[116] He may have been joking, but the point is worth pondering. After a good night's sleep we will find that natural darkness reduces the level of sensory input, as does the relative silence of the hours around dawn. When we rise for prayer, refreshed in mind and relaxed in body, we are less preoccupied with business and more inclined to move into a simple state of communion with God, however this may be expressed.

Giving priority to prayer has an effect on everything that we do. If, in the early morning, we are able to dedicate a solid amount of time to personal prayer, it becomes more likely that moments of prayer will punctuate our working day. In addition, we will often find that insights that come to us during our prayer or holy reading will provide us with the medicine we need not only for ourselves when difficulties arise, but also for those who come to us for help and healing. This is not the purpose of this time, but it is a collateral benefit that helps to bind together our time of prayer and our time of other activities. Our prayer in the dark of night becomes a source of light for our daytime living.

There is another kind of darkness that is more than the absence of light. This is the darkness about which Jesus spoke in the Sermon on the Mount, the darkness that hides our prayer from the gaze of others. "When you pray, enter into your room and close the door, and pray to your Father in secret. And your Father who sees [what is done] in secret will repay you" (Matt. 6:6). When we enter into that secret place we are entering the sphere of God, and in that zone of mysterious darkness in which God so clearly sees us, sometimes we also are permitted to catch an obscure and fleeting glimpse of God.

4. *[Jesus] went out*

To pray well involves departing from where we were. The call to prayer is a summons to set forth, like Abraham, from the familiar land of Ur of the Chaldeans, to march boldly away from the dark slavery of Egypt, to come home from the exile in Babylon. To pray well we also must go forth; we must leave behind what is familiar and, therefore, safe; we must depart from what enslaves us, such as our obligations and, maybe, our work; and from what alienates us and takes us away from ourselves—especially our grievances and our addiction to entertainment. Prayer is a journey into an unknown future in which the certainties of the present are left behind and we are invited to enter into the adventure of a new creation—an adventure that is also a huge insecurity and a risk.

Every journey obliges us to leave something behind. We can carry only so much with us. When I choose to begin a period of prayer, I have to cease doing other things. This means leaving behind not only work but also precious downtime. I make a choice. I also have to move away from thoughts that make me anxious and memories that seize hold of my attention. All of these, to use the words of the fourteenth-century *The Cloud of Unknowing*, must be consigned to the cloud of forgetfulness if we are to pray well. We deliberately expel them from consciousness each time they make an appearance there. Above all we have to let go of our abiding resentments. "When you stand praying let go of anything that you have against someone" (Mk. 11:25). As we advance in years we become aware of how many of our choices are determined by negative feelings stirred up by energies trapped deep within us. We must be continually beginning the process of moving away from those inherent tendencies that make us unhappy and may eventually lead to vice. We will find that the deliberate movement toward prayer is a first step, often repeated, in overcoming the inconsistencies that cause us so much trouble. Prayer is, as Jesus reminds his disciples, the only effective means of liberation from certain kinds of demonic tyranny (Mk. 9:29).

Prayer will often call us to curtail our servitude to functional rationality and to allow ourselves to be guided by the reasons of the heart. Is it not strange that whenever a good inspiration strikes us, we can immediately conjure up a thousand excellent reasons not to follow it? It is as though the head and the heart are at war. Living a spiritual life—especially if we take the Sermon on the Mount as our source of guidance—means living according to a higher rationality. In a sense, it is a kind of madness, because the spiritual option is neither rational nor irrational, but it operates at a deeper level of our being. It does not yield immediate gratification but, instead, promises a more abundant life in the future. This is another way of saying that prayer grows out of faith. Prayer is preeminently a work of faith; without a strong and ever-renewed faith it disappears.

5. *and went away*

Jesus went out and went away: two different verbs. Moving from one place to another is often a means of changing what is happening in consciousness. Saint Benedict's directions about prayer are basic: "If somebody wishes to pray let him simply go in and pray." *Simpliciter intret et oret* (RB 52.4). Thanks to our cavemen ancestors, when we pass through a doorway our awareness switches automatically toward what is ahead. Going to a different place is the most effective way of making a transition from our ordinary life into prayer. Sometimes we can create a buffer zone that provides us with the opportunity consciously to let go of what had been occupying our attention and to orient ourselves toward the upcoming period of prayer. But, whether this is feasible or not, it is very helpful to have a special place for prayer, one that becomes sacred for us, so that simply by entering it we are drawn into an attitude of prayer.

The choice of a place for prayer is a very personal one. Some people prefer a place that is warm, dark, and confined, a womb in which they are enveloped by a prayerful ambience. Others respond best to long vistas and an abundance of light so that they are drawn out of themselves into infinity. Some like a space that is empty; others find it helpful to make use of sacred symbols: images, icons, candles. Some find solace in the presence of the Blessed Sacrament and pray best in a church; others create a little corner of their home to serve as an expression of their faith and a focus for their prayer. Some people find that natural beauty is a good ambience for prayer—and this is especially true when we find ourselves bedeviled by a certain distaste for more explicitly "spiritual" activities.

The lesson is simple and one that most will learn for themselves. Having a habitual place to go to when we pray simplifies the transition into prayer. When we go to that place on a regular basis we will often find that our thoughts follow our footsteps and we move into prayer with greater facility.

6. *to a deserted place*

Jesus goes to a deserted place where solitary communion with the Father is possible. This is a pattern that is visible throughout the Gospel tradition. It is right and proper for Christians to pray together, but the example of Jesus teaches us that there is scope also for solitary prayer, in which we can allow the deepest desires of our heart to come to consciousness without any sense of social constraint or fear of premature interruption.

The desert is the place for apophatic prayer—prayer that is silent and dark, without images or variety, the prayer of quiet attentiveness. Many experience the absence of sensate impressions and the cessation of intellectual operations as emptiness but, in reality, it is far from being a void. When the human spirit is powerfully acted upon by the Holy Spirit, everything else goes into recession. The effect of the Spirit is the opposite of dramatic impact; it is a call to quiet stillness and active receptivity: "Be still and know that I am God" (Ps. 46:10).

The external desert often mirrors our interior disposition. Our prayer may seem dry and desolate, devoid of charm or consolation. This may be because our prayer is in a stage of transition from one mode to another and the familiar indicators no longer exist. This is something a skilled elder can help us to discern. We must also consider the possibility that a desolate prayer is a true indication of the state of our life. The grace of this moment is to see ourselves as we are: whether this be because we are spiritually lazy, morally inconsistent, interiorly divided, or resistant to God's will and impervious to grace. We can hope to discern the cause of our spiritual blankness only by looking calmly at it, asking what message it carries. Perhaps, contrary to our expectations, we will discover within ourselves a source of spiritual energy that wells up from deep inside us and leads us into a moment of intense prayer. It was there all the time, but we discover it only when we take time to allow it to come to the surface. Our prayer will quickly give us a true reading of where we are.

7. *and there he prayed.*

Because we are established in a state of prayer by virtue of our baptism, prayer occurs naturally to the extent that we remove or reduce the habitual impedances to prayer. Prayer is not produced; it is more a matter of alternative activities being reduced. Prayer is more a question of subtraction than of addition. We can get started on prayer simply by going to the place of prayer, leaving behind what normally engages our attention and making room for the Spirit's action. If we think of prayer as a production, there will always be an anxiety of how to procure its elements and fit them together. Much more peace can be found if we think of prayer as simply letting go of everything that occupies our mind and heart at other times, and opening ourselves to the action of God. Sometimes the Spirit will give voice to our deepest desires; sometimes we will bask in the sunshine of God's acceptance and love; sometimes we will become more conscious of our need for forgiveness, healing, renewal, and growth. In whatever form it takes, prayer will always lead us into a fuller truth, but for this to happen, we need to yield control.

Many of the difficulties we create for ourselves in the matter of prayer derive from our failure to recognize that prayer does not have to be generated; it is already with us. We do not have to climb up into the skies or cross the seas to look for it; it is already very close to us. What we have to do is to discover the prayer that is given to us from moment to moment. It is not always the same. It will not always be what we have anticipated. This is because it is not primarily our work, but it is the result of the Holy Spirit working within us, bridging the distance between us and God. Prayer is slowly refashioning our relationship with God, taking us beyond the limits we have imposed on ourselves and leading us into a future we cannot even imagine. As soon as we attempt to take control of our prayer the connection with God weakens, its power to carry us forward is lost, and we are left at the mercy of our own precarious resources. We don't have to stage-manage our prayer, but simply make room for it to happen.

Lord Jesus Christ,
You call us to follow you and to come away
To find you in quiet and hidden places
Where your voice is heard.
Help us to respond to this call
With generosity and perseverance
So that we may receive with open heart
Your gift of more abundant life.
For you are our Lord, for ever and ever. Amen!

CHAPTER NINE

The Grace of Prayer: Contemplation

In the phenomenological study to which we have already referred, Maurice Nédoncelle makes the assertion that all prayer is contemplative; this view is based on the reality that persons praying are convinced that they are in contact with God, and experience this at different levels of their being.[117] When we are in need, we desire to interact with a responsive human person, and not have to deal with computers or blank-faced bureaucrats. In a similar way, when we pray we delight in having a sense that our prayers are received by a real person and not just deposited in a heavenly data bank. Clearly this is not a direct, face-to-face encounter with the all-holy God, but there is real contact at the level of spirit—due to the operation of the Holy Spirit, crying "Abba"—and at the level of faith.[118]

We may think of an example. A simple believer kneels before a statue of the Sacred Heart and says three Hail Marys to Saint Anthony for the resolution of some everyday domestic dilemma. The theology of such an exercise is very tangled, but the fact remains that such prayer is not ineffectual. The person rises from their prayer less troubled, more confident, more at peace. There has been a change within the person. And, furthermore, simple people often find that their prayers are answered.

Perhaps we are inclined to give too much importance to the content of our prayer, turning it into some sort of administrative presentation or request that has to be submitted in the appropriate form. Prayer is the activation of a relationship; it doesn't much matter what form it takes. On one occasion, I capitalized on an opportunity that presented itself to eavesdrop on an elderly couple as they strolled through a public place; they were clearly very close, both physically and emotionally. A transcript of the words they exchanged, however, would not do justice to the depth of their communication. One would begin a sentence and the other would finish it. There was a continuous exchange of comment, not always using words. They were not passing on information; they were celebrating their shared existence. After many decades of life together there was not much new to be said. Their words were simply reaffirmations of the love they shared. This is probably an example of what Ludwig Wittgenstein says in a more complicated way. The inexpressible is inexpressibly contained within what is expressed. Words are important, but they are not the only carriers of messages.

Likewise, our prayer is primarily a celebration of our communion with God; it is not the effort to establish a first contact or to resume a relationship long left in suspense, much less is it the submission of an administrative request. By virtue of our baptism we were freely admitted into the household of God—we became sharers in the divine nature. This is to say that we are confirmed in a state of relationship with God; a state of prayer. As Deuteronomy reminds us, we do not have to cross the seas or go up into the sky to find the means by which we may enter into conversation with God. The opportunity is already to hand. Our prayer does not have to be created; it already exists. We are, at all times, in a state of prayer; the problem is that we are not always conscious of it. The times we set apart for prayer are the times in which we endeavor to become more aware of the state in which we are established by God's grace.

Prayer is not, therefore, primarily a technique: something that can be taught and learned. It is, rather, the effect of a life lived in accordance with the gospel, a life lived in love. Contemplation is—as the Sanskrit meaning of the root *temp* indicates—a state of being in accordance with God, in harmony with God. God is the *temp*late of my life. Like a *temp*le my life is a place on earth that mirrors the heavenly reality. For Saint Bernard contemplation was the natural flow-on from a state of conformity of will—in which progressively, through an ongoing ordering of my affections, my will is becoming more in accordance with God's will. I am moving toward that state exemplified in the life of Jesus, whereby I can begin to say, "My food is to do the will of the One who sent me" (John 4:34). Contemplation is what comes about when our interior division is overcome and we pass into a state in which our heart is substantially undivided—what the ancient monks termed "purity of heart." In this emerging state of transparency God gradually appears. Supposing the window to be clean, it is as though God is outside the window all the time; if we choose to look we can catch sight of the unseeable. Of course, this image limps because God is inside and not outside. The point is, we have to be inclined to look up from what we are doing and gaze through the window of the soul. And sometimes God taps on the window. Contemplation is more something that happens than something that is done.

If contemplation is not a product, then any effort to produce it is futile. The most we can do is not to aim to *produce* contemplation but to invest effort in *reducing* alternative activities. In particular, it involves the cessation of the controlling operation of consciousness. In other words, we have to put our conscious thinking to sleep, to allow the operation of the deeper process of the spirit. This is how the author of *The Cloud of Unknowing* explains this truth, in another book titled *The Epistle of Privy Counsel.*

And well is this work likened to a sleep. For as in sleep the use of the bodily wits is ceased, that the body may take his full rest in feeding and strengthening of the bodily nature: right so in this ghostly sleep the wanton questions of the wild ghostly wits, imaginative reasons, be fast bound and utterly voided, *so that the silly soul may softly sleep* and rest in the lovely beholding of God as he is, in full feeding and strengthening of the ghostly nature.[119]

The basis of all prayer is the presence of "Christ within us: the hope of glory" (Col. 1:27). It is not a matter of knowing or doing but of being. Indwelling prayer is larger than consciousness and so, when no obstacle exists, consciousness is swamped, overcome, swept away. Contemplation is a moment of intensity: in traditional language this is *intentio cordis*.[120] By virtue of his ascension the Word made Flesh is no longer subject to spatiotemporal limitations; he is universally present and accessible—most of all at the level of spirit in the heart of believers.

We do not expect to see God with our bodily eyes—simply because we can sense only what is spatiotemporally limited. We cannot see God by some sort of intellectual vision, because cognition depends on a sensory infrastructure that cannot touch, much less contain divinity. It is only at the level of spirit that God becomes visible. For us to see God we have to leave behind the world of sense, enter the region of unknowing, and allow the Holy Spirit to be our guide. "If we have known Christ Jesus according to the flesh, then we know him thus no longer" (2 Cor. 5:16).

This is why prayer is often described in negative terms such as nakedness, silence, and darkness. Prayer is naked because it admits of no concealment and there is nothing that can be added to it or taken away from it. It is silent because what is communicated cannot be contained in spoken words or intellectual concepts. It is dark because at the level of sense or understanding there is nothing to see; nothing to feel or encompass with our wills. Perhaps there is nothing to experience, in the ordinary meaning of the word. Communion with God is best described as *meta-experiential*: it is something that transcends anything else we do or endure. This is not the same as saying that it is unreal. The contemplative experience belongs to a different order of reality and requires of us a refined sensibility. That is why every tradition of prayer includes the practice of discipline, asceticism, purification, and self-control. The purpose of such exercises is to bring ourselves to the point where we can be fully responsive to the Spirit's leading, and allow ourselves to be drawn toward God. For this to take place a lot of the dross of selfishness must first be burned away and a deep quiet allowed to possess the soul. When much is happening at the conscious level we are too easily attracted away from the dense silence of God. To be content with minimal experience at a level of feeling and consciousness is a prerequisite to being initiated into the subtler states that accompany a deepening experience of God present.

Because we were made for God and in God's image and likeness, and because baptism renders us participant in the very nature of God, then contemplation must be understood not merely as an activity but as a state of being that brings to fulfillment the promise contained in these earlier gifts. It is not something reserved to an elite, but a promise offered to all God's faithful people. In this earthly condition our potential for experiencing the reality of communion with God is limited both by our subjective dispositions and by external factors. As life goes on, however, we often find that the upheaval caused by having to deal with reality becomes somewhat less, and with God's grace it becomes more feasible for us to live in inner harmony. As this happens—and as our environment permits—we begin to catch glimpses of the reality of God's presence, even in situations from which we had thought God would be absent. Moments of contemplative absorption sometimes blossom within "ordinary" prayer, transforming the whole exercise from routine application to a deep but hidden sense of intimacy. The same can happen in the midst of daily activities, usually presupposing that foundations have been laid through regular times of prayer. Such momentary encounters often contain challenge as well as consolation. If we respond positively with the obedience of faith, our powers of spiritual perception will grow; we find that God visits us more frequently when silence reigns in our hearts and even in the course of our everyday activities.

These graced moments of divine intimacy can never be engineered by us; there is always something unpredictable and even whimsical about them. They do not bring us any overt advantage: new ideas or spectacular vistas. In fact, the deeper the experience, the less likely it will be to have obvious fringe benefits. Even our morals will remain unimproved in the short term. Nevertheless, an invisible bonding takes place that slowly cements the human will with that of God. In time this becomes evident in a burgeoning of love; but such a result is not immediate.

The first effect of such an experience is to feel a little out of our depth. Without knowing it we may have moved beyond the zone where ordinary rules apply. To ourselves we may seem to be beyond the pale; those whom we consult may be unable to help; they may be confused by being confronted with what they themselves have never experienced. What is beyond human control is also outside our capacity to understand. What is beyond experience cannot be interpreted and explained in normal language. We have to learn to be content with confidence in divine providence and accept to live in trustful unknowing. We are passive at this moment: God is the one who acts. In the last analysis, we have simply to assent to be led blindly, but we give this trust lovingly and lightly. It cannot be the grudging compliance of a slave. We must learn the art of sitting quietly and waiting for the salvation of the Lord.

The silence into which we are called is not blankness. Silence can be a vibrant expectancy. Gustavo Dudamel, the Venezuelan conductor, has insisted that the silence of a concert audience is an essential and contributory part of every performance. It makes for an experience that is completely different from that of performing in an empty auditorium. And so, our silence in prayer is something worthwhile; it is not nothing. It often gives us a sense of being perched on the precipice of the unknown, attentive, a little apprehensive, but knowing no alternative. Sometimes it seems almost hostile. Just as the desert was traditionally seen not as the spot for a quiet retreat, but a howling wilderness in which demons lived, so God calls us not to rest but, progressively, to a greater fidelity to truth. This closer attachment to ultimate reality is not possible unless we learn to abandon all that is unreal, untrue, and in authentic in our lives. There is a hard-edged quality about the demands of this moment that does not yield to our usual tactics of evasion. We cannot satisfy these demands by telling our story in a different way, highlighting different aspects of our past to accommodate new expectations. God is truth, and if we are to encounter God at the level of spirit we have to leave behind our familiar falsehoods and live by a new law. This is not a matter of shedding obligations and reprogramming our lives. The regime of the Spirit is materially scarcely different from that previously expected of us from outside. Its special characteristic is that it derives its energies from within, not from hope of rewards or the fear of sanctions. It is the law of freedom.

No matter how much we like the word *freedom* the reality can be a little frightening. To become free, we have to allow all binding attachments to be loosed. Freedom is nakedness, according to the ancient maxim, "Naked to follow the naked Christ." For much of our life the rigor of this precept is waived. At a certain point, however, we are suddenly confronted with its exigency. We have lost much, we have been the victims of destructiveness, and now we are called freely to give up the little that remains. It seems so unreasonable. And yet unless we neutralize our paltry possessiveness we will be left in limbo indefinitely. We may ruefully discover that it is easier to be generous in a time of abundance than, like the widow in Mark 12, to give what seems to be our last, pitiable resource. But it is precisely this final and radical act of trust that God requires of us at this time.

In our leaving aside of all temporal hopes we learn to live by a hope that seems hopeless. We no longer have the fig leaves of pretense to cover our native indigence, and somehow we are relieved that we no longer have to keep up appearances. At this point we begin to know what it is to be "poor in spirit." Although this involves nothing less than seeing ourselves as God sees us, we resist the process mightily. As delusions drop off, we become more violently assailed by truth. So it appears. The truth seems mostly bad news. We begin to perceive something of the ugliness and compromise that have disfigured most of our past deeds and still hang around us like a bad smell. Yet, unwelcome though this hard truth be, there is comfort here. Our feet are on the ground. We are touching bottom. Mysteriously, just as God's passion for us is not diminished by our sinfulness, so this new vision of our need for God makes us share a little of God's unconditional love for ourselves. What a surprise! The more we see the unwelcome truth about ourselves through God's eyes, the more accepting we become of our own reality. Our love and self-esteem increase, because, now, even our self-love is shaped by God.

There is a fire that burns beneath these gray ashes that are all that remains of human achievement. Beneath the dullness there is an emergent passion. The dim light is not twilight but dawn. To have penetrated to the heart and to have found freedom there does not offer much consolation at the level of emotion or intellect, but it carries its own subtle legitimation. We no longer feel inclined to go back to mental fireworks or powerful experiences, because somehow they have lost their appeal. They can be left aside as means that have served their purpose and are no longer needed. As Thomas Merton wrote, "Contemplative prayer is, in a way, simply the preference for the desert, for emptiness, for poverty."[121] Far from being a "problem" in prayer, such aridity—given the presence of other authenticating signs—can be the entrance into an interior state that progressively transforms the whole person. Especially in the early phases of it, there is a certain malaise, a nostalgia for the past and a desire to "fix things," even though one dimly senses that nothing is broken. This is a crucial point when a decision has to be taken concerning who is in charge. If it is to be God, then back off. Let God act.

At times one may have experiences that are a little esoteric. There may be moments of intense absorption when one seems to disappear and return without knowing exactly where one has been. At times the body may join unbidden in the dance of prayer or there may be some overflowing into one's inner sensibility. Other effects may be more habitual such as a certain detachment from what we have come to see as the trivialities of daily life. Having touched the essential, be it ever so briefly, one's taste for the banal is permanently damaged.

Mostly, however, it is a matter of persevering with the low-impact landscape of quiet prayer and following our ordinary, obscure, and laborious round. Perhaps we are conscious of an elusive awareness that backgrounds our activities like a half-remembered melody. One moment it is there; the next it flits away like a shy little bird that knows we are looking at it. The most immediate demand is that we do not lose faith in God's leading of us. We are not to curtail our devotion because it seems to accomplish nothing. As *The Cloud of Unknowing* recommends, "Keep on doing this nothing."[122] This is the ultimate detachment to which we are called, that we give ourselves to "nothing" in preference to every other possibility. This takes grit. Thus, Julian of Norwich places this exhortation in the mouth of Christ.

> Pray with your whole being even though you think that it has no savor for you. For such prayer is very profitable even though you feel nothing. Pray with your whole being, though you feel nothing, though you see nothing, even though it seems impossible to you. It is in dryness and in barrenness, in sickness and in feebleness that your prayer is most pleasing to me, even though you think that it has little savor for you.[123]

At this stage one has moved away from concern with doing. One is content to be. Such attention to being is, of course, more than drowsy indolence or daydreaming. It is a moment in which all one's energies are concentrated in a single intense stream—like a laser. Far from being insulated from the immediate environment—drugged out of reality by religion, as it were—there is a high degree of personal presence to concrete existence. In a certain sense the contemplative act is like stepping out of space and time. The inner space and duration of such experiences have no relation with the spatiotemporal shell in which they occur. There is a concentrated awareness of the totality of our experiences—including those we would rather forget—though these are not the object of our attention but, as it were, the matrix by which the experience is shaped. We are not looking at ourselves, but are yet aware that every atom of our historical being is involved in the encounter toward which we are moving.

When we step outside space-time, we step inside God. We view God from within, as it were—not as an object outside ourselves. Relationship has become intimacy; intimacy has become identification—so the mystics tell us. Because our whole being is a participation in the being of God, when we become fully present to our essential selves we discover that to live means to move deeper into the Mystery of God. Of us it can be said as it is said of the Word in Saint John's Prologue, that we also are "toward God." Still on earth, still involved with persons and projects, still manifestly imperfect, yet relentlessly on the move toward God.

Another way of expressing this supreme paradox is to say that in contemplative prayer God ceases to be the object of our prayer, but becomes its subject. God is the one who prays in us. Our prayer is our participation in the prayer of Christ. Having the mind of Christ, to use Saint Paul's phrase (1 Cor. 2:16; Phil. 2:5), means that we enter into Christ's subjectivity. So conformed is our will to his that when we say "I" we mean "Christ." "I live now not I, but Christ lives in me" (Gal. 2:20; see Phil. 1:21). When we gaze toward the Father, we see through Christ's eyes. Our attitudes to human beings are imprinted with those of Christ: compassion, understanding, self-offering. In a mysterious way, we become most fully ourselves by "putting on Christ" (Gal. 3:27; Rom. 13:14).

Such prayer often becomes more Trinitarian as time goes on. Prayer assumes different emphases. There are occasions in which one is powerfully aware of being drawn toward the Father: desire, aspiration, a stretching forth at the level of being. At other times one is more aware of the impulsion of the Holy Spirit; one is possessed by a force and a love not one's own that pushes one beyond normal limits. It is the Spirit that spans the chasm between us and the Father (Rom. 8:26) and teaches us to call out *Abba* (Gal. 4:5–6; Rom. 8:15). Most often, perhaps, our experience of prayer seems centered on identification or solidarity with Jesus the Word or, in a wider sense, it is experienced as communion with the Church, with the saints, with the Mother of the Lord, with all humanity—even with the whole cosmos. These experiences can coincide, for they are not mutually exclusive, but it is normal for one or other to claim precedence in our limited consciousness at different times in our life.

Such prayer, grounded as it is in truth, has a curiously refreshing character about it. Stepping back from the tyranny of time renews youthfulness (Ps. 103:5; Isa. 40:31) and helps us regain that character of childlike simplicity that was so favored by Jesus (Mk. 10:14–15). At the other end of the scale, contemplation gives a wisdom that surpasses age or experience, as is demonstrated in the biblical examples of Samuel and Daniel and others. In the book of Revelation the risen Lord is presented as the one who renews and restores creation (Rev. 21:5). "If anyone is in Christ, a new creation takes place" (2 Cor. 5:17; see Gal. 6:15). We are as newborn babes (2 Pet. 2:2). Our transparency is restored, and we begin to reflect the likeness of God, in whose image we were created. In some inchoative way, the expectation of the whole created order has been realized.

This dark encounter with God returns us to the innocence lost when the gates of Eden slammed behind us: not merely to the guileless incapacity for evil that we see in children but to a sage and stable preference for what is good and true. Knowing good and evil, by the power of God's grace we opt for good so radically that any previous wavering is set at naught. Happy are those who see God, for they shall become clean of heart! This paradoxical restoration explains why God is described in one of the ancient collects of the Roman liturgy as "the restorer and lover of innocence." How illogical! Innocence is such that its charm consists in never having been lost. Once squandered it is impossible to recover.

Yes, God's action is illogical. In fact, illogicality and impossibility are the hallmarks of divine intervention (Gen. 18:14; Lk. 1:37). In contemplative prayer the innocence that we have lost is given back to us intact. Our sins are remitted: not merely overlooked, ignored, excused, or even forgiven, but entirely negated. God's act of salvation transcends time. The damage we have inflicted on ourselves is neutralized. This is truly regeneration; no sign of our former degeneracy remains. In the contemplative experience we realize in fact the potential inherent in baptism. Between our initiation into God and its culmination there *seems* to be a delay while the residues of sin are burnt out and the fires of charity are fanned into flame. However, this impression owes more to the distortion brought about by our perception of time than to the reality of God's act. God's definitive saving of us needs to be described in the present tense. God is eternally creating us, conserving us, redeeming us. If we perceive something of this simultaneity, then this is the fruit of the Spirit working within us. Our efforts to live a "spiritual life" simply confirm that something greater than human action is operating within us.

Contemplative prayer is certainly the summit of Christian life; it is the goal to which we all tend. It is the ordinary outcome of a life of fidelity to basic Christian imperatives; it operates even when the person is unaware of the gift received. Many simple persons of faith frequent this sanctuary without knowing the name of what they experience. There is nothing exclusive about it—except that it seems reserved to the small and humble, to those who do not deserve it. There is certainly nothing glamorous about contemplation: there is nothing in it that can be translated into marketable commodities and subsequently traded for some temporal advantage. Contemplation is entirely gratuitous, pure grace: on God's part, total gift; on ours, total receptivity. The Word became flesh to be with us. He called us to join him so that we might, together with the whole human family, consecrate our lives to this lifelong journey that carries us toward God.

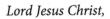

Lord Jesus Christ,

*When you called us to baptism you called us to share in
your divine life.*

Help us to withdraw from the tumult of worldly involvement

*And to respond to the voice of the Holy Spirit crying "Abba"
within us.*

*May we be one with you, adoring the Father in Spirit and
in truth*

for ever and ever. Amen!

CHAPTER TEN

The Grace of Faith

A ll religious practice is an expression of the belief that we exist in a state of dependence on an ultimate and absolute reality that is outside our sphere of being and, therefore, outside our direct experience. As a result, none of us can give a completely convincing account of religion in terms of "secular" rationality. What we hold to be true and imperative in thought and word and action will seem to others as foolish or scandalous. Almost inevitably they will say that, because of our faith, we are allocating a measure of importance to an unseen world for which there is no "scientific" evidence. We do not deny this. Religion is rightly considered to be "out of this world," but that does not mean that it is unreal, nor does it prove that there is no objective reality that corresponds to our basic premises. When we say that God exists it is probably more correct to understand this as meaning that God is per se Being, rather than one Being among many; this truth makes silence about God more accurate and perhaps more eloquent than speech. We may not be able to engage in discourse about God that is comprehensible to nonbelievers, but this is not necessarily an indication that what we say is untrue. Can you explain color to one who is blind or music to one who is deaf? There is more to the universe than we humans can perceive directly. Bats hear what we cannot, and dogs can smell what we cannot, and eagles can see what we cannot. The unperceived is not necessarily nonexistent.

Our having received the gift of faith should not lead us to complacency. We who practice religion should not consider ourselves untouched by the secular skepticism that surrounds us. Unbelief infects us. Our faith, perhaps without our knowing it, is not absolute. More often than not our understanding of it is qualified, partial, and undeveloped, and so our assent is incomplete. For example, we will often find ourselves buttressing our presentation of religion by appealing to its visible benefits; its works of compassion and education, its ethical and moral guidance, its role in personal well-being. So eloquent are we in religion's defense that we may convince even ourselves that its principal value is to be found in these collateral benefits. And meanwhile we become forgetful of the "supernatural" basis of all our faith and practice.

It is possible to admire Jesus as a great teacher of wisdom and as a model of genuine humanity and, with great sincerity of heart, to become his enthusiastic followers on purely rational or historical grounds—just as some may become followers of Socrates, the Buddha, or Karl Marx. Such an adherence is not what Christian discipleship is about. Christianity is more than an identification with an admired leader; it is not merely a philosophy or a code of conduct. Authentic Christianity sees itself as a participation in the life of God through immersion in the mystery of the Word become flesh. At the heart of our adherence to Christ is a truth that surpasses human understanding, one that even we, who accept the truth, cannot fully explain. The gift of faith takes us beyond the known world into a sphere of being that transcends the power of rational thought. "Now faith is the assurance of things hoped for, the conviction of things not seen" (Heb. 11:1).

Faith is what connects us to the invisible world that is the sphere of God. It does this in a manner that gives us a measure of certainty, even though there is no sensory or rational evidence to support it. Faith does not lead us to admit a mere possibility or a probability; it convinces us of the reality of the unseen as if it had appeared bodily before our eyes—though, obviously, there are degrees of faith. As far as sense and reason are concerned faith is darkness, but that darkness is merely the shadow cast by a brighter light that shines at the level of spirit. Faith is not a perception or a deduction that is brought into the human heart from outside, but it is an outburst of divine energy at the very center of personal being that initially has no connection with what is outside. Faith moves outward from this center in the course of a lifetime: touching our experience, energizing our faculties of intellect and will, moderating our behavior, even transforming our outward appearance, and, thus, through us reaching out to bring the Good News to all creation.

The initial gift of faith occurs below the level of consciousness. Perhaps it is imparted at the very dawn of reflexive self-consciousness. There it remains active but latent, perhaps for many years, perhaps for many decades. It awaits some external herald, whom it will instinctively recognize, who will call it into visibility and action. In this context, we might be reminded of Saint Paul's preaching in the Areopagus: "What you unknowingly worship, I make known to you" (Acts 17:23). The Church's proclamation of the Good News has the effect of giving outward form to what is already inwardly if secretly experienced. Preaching the gospel has as its purpose the bringing together of the inner and personal dynamic of the gift of faith with its outward and corporate expression. This conjunction allows the object of faith to be named and, with the help of revelation, to be described, understood, and shared.

The reality to which we give the name *faith* is richly layered. I have already mentioned this. There are five moments to be distinguished in the act of faith, similar to those evidenced in conversion or vocation.

1. an *experience* with a more or less strong affective component,
2. an illumination of the *mind* of more or less clarity—this was the topic of Pope Francis's encyclical *Lumen fidei*—
3. an assent of the *will* of more or less potency,
4. a translation of this assent into daily *practice* of more or less consistency, and
5. a lifelong *perseverance* in belief, trust, and practice.

Faith is trust or confidence in God, faith is belief, and faith is fidelity, commitment, and perseverance. Faith is not the skeletal reality we sometimes assume it to be. Quite the contrary! The faith that works through love is a rich and all-embracing participation in the life of God. That is why it is called a "theological virtue."

In many persons the gift of faith remains underground. These are those whom we may see as the "anonymous Christians" about whom Karl Rahner wrote, the people who live good lives in accordance with the inner voice of conscience, but who have never had the opportunity to link this inner call to integrity of life with the outward forms of organized Christianity.[124] "How, then, can they call upon one in whom they have not believed? How can they believe in one of whom they have not heard? How can they hear unless someone proclaims [the Good News to them]?" (Rom. 10:14). "Faith desires instruction," writes Saint Augustine.[125] When the believer externalizes and objectivates faith, it becomes possible for graced unbelievers to recognize in this external form the secret something that has always guided their conduct, and so they are able to attach their deep personal aspirations to a common creed and code of conduct. In the process of "conversion" they discover what they have always been looking for in an already-existing form. And not only that. By continuing to explore this external formulation of faith and

making it their own, they discover more than an extrinsic richness; they find new treasure in what they had always cherished
and obeyed.

Faith is the origin and the ongoing engine of all spiritual life.
It is God's gratuitous gift to us, but to produce its fruits it calls for
a response. We are obliged to render what Saint Paul calls "the
obedience of faith" (Rom. 1:5; 16:26). This obedience leads to the
works of faith about which the Epistle of James writes: "What
profit is there, my brothers, if someone claims to have faith but has
no works? Is such a faith able to save? . . . Faith by itself, if it has
no works, is dead. . . . You see that a person is justified by works
and not by faith alone. . . . Just as the body without the spirit is
dead, so faith without works is dead" (Jas. 2:14, 17, 24, 26). Faith,
although interior, is living and active; it cannot be without impact
on how we experience life or how we respond to its opportunities
and challenges. It is in responding to the gift of faith that we open
our lives to God.

Faith is our connection with God. The first and fundamental
work of faith is to actualize that connection. We do this especially
by prayer in all its forms: by listening with the ear of the heart to
God's word, by joining in the communal prayer of God's faithful
people, by seeking God in solitude and silence. Faith without
works is dead; faith without prayer is dying. The other good works
that follow faith depend for their efficacy on this vital link. We
may believe that we can do the works of God without reference to
God, and it may be that God may permit this autonomous functioning to produce good effects for a time, but we will eventually
discover that relying exclusively on our own resources eventually
undermines our best efforts and may even bring us to the point of
personal crisis. Because we have replaced God with self, when the
self reaches its limits and begins to fail, we begin to doubt not self
(as we ought), but God. We have forgotten God, and that is the
cause of many of our troubles.

Faith is our point of contact with the invisible world of spirit. It may well seem like a tenuous connection, but it is the beginning of something greater. One image I have of faith is something I have not experienced personally but only seen in films. When a transfer is to be made between two ships in rough seas, first a thin cord is shot from one ship across the intervening space until it lands on the deck of the other. Then progressively heavier ropes are attached and pulled across until it is possible to connect the two ships by a stout cable. Faith may seem, at the beginning, a very slight link with God. If it is allowed to do what it can do, it will become stronger and the connection with God will become more robust.

Faith is our means of communication with the sphere of existence that is beyond space and time. The immediate effect of this link with God is to impart to us an assured hope. We become confident in the unseen energy of God, which is able to achieve good results that are beyond human anticipation. We work hard and we do our best, but we are often made aware that God's grace going before us and following after us is the principal agent in producing good results. Even now God is at work in our midst. How much more should we look forward to the complete and final fulfillment of God's promises, confident that, in the end, all will be well. "For it is in hope we were saved. But hope that is seen is not hope. Who hopes for what he sees? But if we hope for what we do not see, we wait for it by patience" (Rom. 8:24–25).

Hope is the particular need for those who endure hardship. Physical pain, emotional disturbance, bereavement, mental confusion, misunderstanding, rejection, persecution, and remorseless demands necessarily limit the horizons of our perception so that we cannot see beyond our immediate labor or distress. Our objective suffering is often increased by a sense of the apparent hopelessness of our situation and the dimness of our future prospects. It may well be true that in this world we are troubled, but we can find peace, as the martyrs did, by raising our eyes and allowing faith to generate hope within our troubled hearts so that we endure without becoming dispirited.

> Therefore, since we have been justified through faith, we have peace with God through our Lord Jesus Christ, through whom we have gained access by faith into this grace in which we stand. And we boast in the hope of the glory of God. Not only so, but we also boast in our troubles, because we know that trouble brings about patience, patience brings about character, and character brings about hope. And hope does not disappoint us, because God's love has been poured out in our hearts by the Holy Spirit, whom he has given to us. (Rom. 5:1–5)

All prayer begins with the faith-inspired hope for something better. It may be that from the midst of suffering we pray for relief. We may pray for deliverance from harm, for healing from illness, or for temporal benefits of which we stand in need. We may enter into prayer in the hope of consolidating or deepening our union with God. There are many points of entry for prayer, but all of them derive from our neediness. I have already quoted the text of Saint Augustine: "Because I am human, therefore I am weak; because I am weak, therefore I pray." As the psalms of lamentation illustrate, prayer frequently begins with an evocation of our troubles, lifting them up to God in a spirit of supplication, but, more often than not, it then moves on to an expression of confidence in God's imminent help and thence to thanksgiving for deliverance. Negative experience is often the beginning of our prayer. Faith allows us gradually to perceive our troubles in a different light. Instead of obstacles to union with God, the difficulties that brought us to prayer begin to bind us more fully to God's merciful love so that whether we are delivered from them or not, they cease to have the power to block our awareness of God's fatherly concern for our ultimate welfare.

Prayer habitually begins with a particular agenda derived from the situation in which we find ourselves. Often that remains the ongoing ambience in which prayer occurs; it is the interaction of faith with the external or internal reality of our lives. Sometimes it moves on from there to become a prayer of pure faith, in which nothing happens or, at least, we are conscious of nothing happening. We feel as though we are suspended between heaven and earth. We have temporarily laid aside earthly concerns and preoccupations, but we are not aware of our minds and hearts being filled with heavenly realities. There is no content and yet no sense of emptiness, a bareness that is not barrenness, a light that is invisible, a presence that is imperceptible. During the time of prayer, we may not be aware of much happening, beyond our batting away distractions and struggling to remain alert and focused. Nevertheless, after prayer we may feel, in a vague sort of way, that our time was well spent, but we will not be able to say exactly what the benefits were.

Prayer is best when we are no longer in control of its content, even though our active contribution seems limited to not cutting it short, not abandoning it for something that seems more comfortable or more useful. Prayer could almost be defined as a period in which we deliberately give up control—and maybe that is why we are so reluctant to engage in it. Our task in prayer is to provide a time and place for the unexpected to happen and to push aside everything that causes our attention to waver. The Holy Spirit is the principal agent in generating prayer; we merely make room for the Spirit's action. "The Spirit comes to the help of our weakness. We do not know how to pray as we ought, but the Spirit makes intercession for us with wordless sighs" (Rom. 8:26). The Spirit prompts a sigh (or groan): an expiration of breath from the depths of our being, expressing an emotion that is too complex for words. A sigh can be the bearer of our frustration or despair; it can equally express desire and yearning. It does not have to be reduced to rational categories. The Spirit's breathing becomes our breath, and then it comes forth from deep inside us to seek its resolution in God. By the action of the Holy Spirit the distance between us and God is bridged. We cannot accomplish this by our own resources; we are totally reliant on grace. Our task is to attain a state of active and receptive passivity, to allow the Spirit to act. Sometimes the Spirit inspires us with words, gathered from our lectio divina or from the liturgy, that seem to embody what we wish to cast upon God. At other times, there is silence: a deep attention that holds us, but without any tangible content. Under the Spirit's guidance our prayer may even open out into a yawning abyss of misery that cries out wordlessly for mercy. Prayer is best when we are no longer in control of what happens; it is the Holy Spirit who is at work.

It is by faith that we allow the Spirit to act in us. This means that whenever we take up the task of prayer we do well to spend a moment reminding ourselves of its essential dynamic, as it were, waking up our faith. This means that often we can begin our prayer not only by a conscious act of recollection, but also by calling on the Holy Spirit to teach us how we are to pray on this day and at this moment. We always come to prayer as amateurs. The prayer of yesterday has expired. We have to discover today's prayer, derived as it is from our situation at this moment and, mysteriously, preparing us for what will happen next. We are very unwise to go to prayer with distinct expectations; when we come to prayer we enter a zone of radical uncertainty because the initiative belongs to God alone.

Uncertainty is abhorrent to us because it implies waiting without having anything concrete to do to improve the situation. If our prayer fails even to begin, we are inclined to see it as a failure, as time wasted. This is a false perception. The uncertainty derives from the fact that prayer is a mirror that portrays us as we are and, because we lack self-knowledge, we are fearful of it. Prayer is always "successful" because what happens during the time of prayer is a truthful expression of the state of our life. If our experience is one of boredom, impatience, and rebellion, then this is how we really are, beneath our good works and our self-engineered persona. Prayer gets to the heart of the matter; it is not convinced by our image-making and press releases. What we are in prayer, we are in fact. If what we see in prayer is displeasing then maybe we ought to do something to change ourselves; it is no good throwing out the mirror; it is, in the final analysis, our best friend.

The way we deal with the dread that prayer sometimes arouses in us is to enter fully into it, to make the experience of uneasiness and tedium the starting point of our prayer. Instead of denying the reality of the darkness into which we are plunged, we accept it as an insufficiently recognized truth about ourselves and, like the publican praying in the temple, we use it as a means of access to God: "O God, be merciful to me a sinner." Now we are standing in the truth. We do not deny that, by grace, we practice virtue and, perhaps, do God's work. We do not fail to recognize that the Almighty has done great things for us. Nevertheless, with sincere conviction, we affirm our belief that all our goodness is precarious and that we are wholly reliant on the bounty of God's love and mercy.

Our faith is a gift from God, and when it penetrates our life experience it gives rise to prayer—but this does not happen easily. Nearly always there are barriers that render the transition into prayer difficult. Consider the woman cured of chronic hemorrhages in Mark 5:25–34. Long-term illness carries its own temptation to despair of improvement, and in this case the woman had impoverished herself by seeking all kinds of medical aid. In addition, the woman was considered ritually unclean and, so, forbidden to approach people; Jesus was surrounded by a bustling crowd that made direct access to him almost impossible; and the

woman herself was burdened with fear of the possible consequences
of her action. So many reasons to do nothing, so many arguments
in favor of continuing the status quo, yet something impelled her
to risk doing something new. Jesus names this hidden dynamism
"faith": "Your *faith* has saved you." The boldness of faith is what
enables us to transcend the obstacles between us and prayer, to
reach out to touch and to be made whole and clean. The obstacles
that prevent each of us from making contact with Jesus are
different and distinctive. We need to identify them so that we can
get beyond them—not by employing our own resources, but by
unleashing the power of faith, bringing it to bear on our difficulties
and resistances and using these as springboards to prayer. We
remember that Satan, as his name indicates, is primarily an
accuser—one who keeps reminding us of our own unworthiness
and using this not as an incentive to approach the throne of grace
but as a deterrent to our continuing in discipleship. As in martial
arts, we use the opponent's own momentum against him. When
we are disturbed by adversity and a sense of unworthiness, instead
of seeking to return to normality, we can use the disturbance as an
incentive to prayer. We pray because we are upset.

The gift of faith is also the gift of prayer. When I recognize
that the gift of faith is the beginning of our prayer, I am affirming
that the possibility of prayer begins with God and not with myself.
Taking this for granted means that my efforts to pray will largely
involve the cessation of activities rather than attempting to do or
achieve something specific by myself. "Be still and know that I am
God." "Speak, Lord, for your servant is listening."

Loving Father,
In calling us to faith
You call us also to prayer.
Give us the courage to seek your presence every day,
Especially in times of darkness, difficulty, and indifference.
Keep us faithful to the gift we have received.
We ask this through Christ our Lord. Amen!

The Grace of Revelation

Revelation is the counterpart of faith. If we understand faith as our opening to the unseen spiritual world, then revelation is God's coming to meet us in an act of self-manifestation. When we move more deeply into the spiritual zone then we begin to experience something of the transcendent attractiveness and lovableness of God. This is not so much a rational encounter with an abstract Absolute, as finding ourselves drawn willy-nilly beyond the world of ordinary experience into a strange sense of divine love entering into us.

We do not possess the vocabulary to describe a spiritual encounter, whether it occurs as the inauguration of our journey with God, or as it is repeated in later graced moments. Words drawn from the world of sensory experience fail lamentably to encapsulate what has occurred interiorly. We must resort to poetry or images if we are not to remain forever silent. These attempts to describe what we have experienced are, inevitably, subjective: clothing what is essentially beyond comprehension with more familiar elements drawn from deep within our own psyche—using words, concepts, and feelings. We have encountered Mystery and we find ourselves drawn into its depths, and, in that moment, we feel more fully alive; but we find ourselves unable to explain what is happening beyond trite and conventional terms that, even to our own ears, sound hollow.

Without words we cannot conceptualize what has occurred; we cannot so easily relate it to everyday experience. This being the case, we cannot make the connections that will enable what we have experienced to influence the everyday choices we make. Without words it is difficult to share our experience with others who might guide us in its interpretation. Unless what we have seen can take form in our thoughts and in our actions, our encounter with the spiritual world remains nebulous: a one-off spiritual event in a life otherwise wholly dedicated to this-worldly pursuits.

An experience deemed "spiritual" is known by its energy-imparting character, such that it cannot be explained directly through the electrical or biochemical activities of the brain, nor by the interplay of natural phenomena, nor through some psychological quirk. The sphere of God is not a parallel universe but exists in relationship with our own. Spiritual world and material world interact. This everyday world of space and time exists inside the eternity of the spiritual world, in a state of total dependence. God created our world. God conserves it in existence. God will bring it to its fulfillment. If we care to ponder the nature of this relationship, we already begin to know something of the existence of a Higher Power. This is not a truth obvious to an unthinking person; but to one who reflects deeply the existence of God is knowable. It is evident only to the wise, as Aquinas notes: *per se notum quoad sapientes tantum.* God's existence is revealed only to those who take the time to consider at depth the world around them.

Saint Paul admits this principle clearly in the first chapter of his Epistle to the Romans. He is speaking about what happens if we allow ourselves to drift away from the experience of God, how our spiritual faculties become degraded to the extent that conscience is disabled and, as a result, our behavior becomes bestial.[126] The converse of what he is saying may be implied. It is possible for us to know the Creator through what has been created, and this experiential knowledge has the effect of heightening our inward perception, of giving us access to the spiritual world and, thereby, beginning the process of upgrading our behavior. Thus, we begin to act in a more fully human manner, less subject to the control of subpersonal instincts and impulses. In the mind of Saint Paul, the unbelief and immorality of the pagans is inexcusable because, although they did not have access to the gift of the Mosaic law, they were able, if they so willed, to extend their intellectual and moral horizons beyond the visible and so attain to the ultimate principle of the universe. The world around us is not totally opaque; there are moments of translucence in which we glimpse darkly a Mystery toward which we feel ourselves drawn.

Saint Thomas Aquinas spoke of five ways in which believers might assure themselves that their faith in the existence of God was not irrational. These are not so much apodictic proofs as supportive buttresses for what we believe: the content of faith is not unreasonable. Reasoning can support faith but it cannot replace it. Something needs to happen at a deeper level of experience. The act of faith is closer to wonder than to an intellectual conclusion. It is something simple and childlike, yet very profound. For many persons the first intimation of transcendent reality comes through their experience of beauty, in one form or another.[127] The apprehension of something beautiful has the effect of taking us out of ourselves; it is an ecstatic experience. We are moved by our experience of beauty: captivated, enraptured, enchanted. There is a certain potency in the experience that can cause us henceforth to see the world in a different light.

God has created us with a prevenient receptivity to divine revelation in whatever form it manifests itself. It can come through the book of nature or the book of inner experience. Enlightenment can result from the inspiring words or example of another person, which hold up to us a mirror in which we catch sight of our own infinite potentiality and are drawn to fulfill it. In so many ways can we be led beyond ourselves into infinity—but for many of us this transition from visible to invisible is too difficult. We tend to go no further than the initial delight we experience. So it was, that God needed to speak to us in a more explicit, less subtle form.

We are not merely philosophers; we are "a people of the Book." At the heart of Christianity is the claim that God has spoken to us through words as well as by the silent language of creation and, in so doing, has manifested in human terms something of the inaccessible light of divinity. Through the life-giving precepts of the Mosaic law, through the inspired utterances of the prophets, and through the wisdom of the sages, God has spoken to humankind in various manners. At the end of the ages, God's self-revelation has reached a climax in the incarnation of God's Word, the Son of God made flesh and dwelling in our midst, like us in all things except sin. Henceforth religion is not something generated by our own initiative, or something that is merely the expression of our own experiences and aspirations. It is a response to what has been gratuitously given. We now gain access to spiritual reality by receiving within ourselves the divine self-revelation and allowing it slowly to refashion our lives in its own likeness. But this re-creation will occur only to the extent that we permit it, to the extent that we offer hospitality to the word of revelation. We must understand that the gift of the word involves an obligation; the ever-present self-revelation of God is also a commandment that is meant to guide our daily lives. The gift is a summons to new life; we receive the gift by responding to the call and living in accordance with what has been made possible for us. There is no excuse: the word has been to given us, it is accessible; our task is to put it into practice.

> Now this commandment that I am commanding you this day is not too difficult for you or far away. It is not in the sky, so that you say, "Who will go up into the sky to fetch it for us so that we may hear it and observe it?" Nor is it across

the sea, so that you say, "Who will cross the sea to fetch it for us so that we may hear it and observe it?" No, the word is very close to you; it is in your mouth and in your heart so you may observe it. (Deut. 30:11–14)

The historic word of revelation was audible, it could be written down, it could be passed from one person or generation to another, it has been translated into various languages; but it is not a thing. It is force, a power, a dynamism. "The word of God is living and active, sharper than every two-edged sword. It penetrates even to the division of soul and spirit, joints and marrow; and it judges the thoughts and dispositions of the heart" (Heb. 4:12). The word of revelation is not merely an external word that provides us with information. God's word is a power for salvation that links up with something within us and draws forth from our depths a latent desire to make contact with God.

We experience the power of God's word through its effects within us. According to Psalm 19:7–8, there are four ways in which divine revelation impacts us:

1. It revives the soul.
2. It gives wisdom to the simple.
3. It gives joy to the heart.
4. It gives light to the eyes.

The Word of God gives us vitality, wisdom, joy, and illumination. By it we become fully alive. There is a mysterious affinity between the Word and the deepest recesses of our being, so that the Word generates an echo in our hearts that finds expression in a desire for a more intense relationship with God. The Word helps us to become aware of our latent desire for God and to name it. The "authority" of the Word results from its being authenticated from deep inside. Our whole being recognizes the longed-for truth of what is presented to us and cries out, "Amen!" Surely this is how the crowds responded to the words of Jesus. They said, "He teaches with authority." They felt that Jesus was giving verbal expression to the truth already present deep within them.

God's Word is sown in our hearts so that our desire for God may grow and increase. But we must welcome the implanted word in humility and docility. "Receive with meekness the implanted Word, for it has power to save your souls" (Jas. 1:21). That we are admonished to take care to welcome the Word implies that there are dangers to be avoided. In the explanation given by the Evangelist Mark to Jesus's parable about the sower and the seed, three situations are envisaged that impede our reception (Mk. 4:13–19). In the first, our resistance to the Good News is threatened by the suggestions of Satan, the accuser, who undermines our confidence in the goodness of God and attempts to overwhelm the good seeds of hope with the darnel of despair. In the second, faith is undermined by troubles and persecutions—it is not sufficiently buttressed by patience and endurance. In the third, we are unable to receive the word because of worldly cares, the lure of riches, and other uncontrolled desires. For the word to be fruitful these obstacles must be neutralized so that the word is received with understanding (Matt. 13:23) and patience (Lk. 8:14).

There has been a tendency, especially in the West, to make of divine revelation an object—something that can be isolated, analyzed, defined, and protected. Its primary function however is subjective, to bring real men and women to conversion, to offer them a new perceptual horizon against which they can measure their lives. The word takes its cue from the situation of those to whom it is addressed. The word of God is the proclamation of the Good News. It is successful when people have a change of heart and begin to live in fidelity to the gospel. The spoken word is incomplete until it is heard. It is only when many faithfully share this grace that a *sensus fidelium* begins to emerge—an orthodoxy and an orthopraxy that can be given "objective" formulation so that they may serve as a guide and principle of discernment. Revelation was not meant first to be frozen in formulas; first it acts as an agent of change in the lives of real people and communities, and only then can its parameters be defined.

Our approach to revelation must be interactive. For in God's self-manifestation we come to learn not only about God but also about ourselves. We discover something of our hidden selves. According to Saint Athanasius, the Scriptures serve as a mirror in which we become aware of the movements of the soul.[128] We were created, as Karl Rahner insisted, as "hearers of the Word."[129] By listening we acquire the spiritual self-knowledge that leads us to comprehend that our existence is one of total dependence on God. If we try to live autonomously, failure and frustration will soon show us our limits. What we learn from revelation is that we are made for God, we subsist within God's providence, and our fulfillment will come through an ever-closer relationship with God. Self-knowledge of this kind leads us to prayer.

"Receive with meekness the implanted word, for it has power to save your soul." When Saint James speaks of God's word as "implanted" he is saying that we must make every effort to internalize the word. Revelation is not meant to be an external code of behavior, a set of by-laws to govern every moment of the day. Rather, the word aims at creating a new heart, one that is responsive to the presence of God. We must allow the word to re-form our beliefs and values in such a way that we begin to act as Christ acted. We read Scripture, we allow it to speak to our hearts, in order that we may become other Christs.

Since the time of Origen of Alexandria in the third century, different levels of meaning have been distinguished in the Scriptures.[130] The obvious meaning he named the "literal" or "historical" sense of the text. This is somewhat accessible to any casual reader and can be further investigated even by an unbelieving scholar. Beyond this, however, is a world of meaning that becomes apparent only under the radiance of faith. The word of Scripture gives greater depth to the understanding of the truth that follows faith. It serves as a guide to a more Christlike manner of acting and reacting. It stirs up the gift of prayer within us and lifts up our hearts to God. If we read Scripture only as a narrative or as a source of information we are missing out on these more profound and existential resonances that the inspired text is meant to produce in the heart of the believer. Listen to Saint Bernard of Clairvaux, who sees reading Scripture as a form of spiritual nourishment: we do not live on bread alone, but on every word that proceeds from the mouth of God.

> What is the meaning of the expression, "Those who love me will keep my words?" . . . Keep the word of God in the same way as you would preserve bodily food. For the word of God is a living bread and food for the mind. So long as earthly food is stored in a box it can be stolen or nibbled by mice, or it can go bad if it is left too long. But if you eat the food you do not have to worry about any of these. This is the way to preserve God's word. Blessed are they who keep it! Let it pass into the innards of your soul, and then let it make its way into your feelings and into your behavior. Eat well and your soul will delight in the abundance. Do not forget to eat your bread lest your heart dry up, but let your soul be filled as with a banquet.[131]

Elsewhere Bernard uses an unlovely image of the relationship between attentive reading of the Scriptures and prayer. What is prayer? Prayer is like a belch that follows a hearty meal. The Latin word he uses is *eructatio*, and it brings to mind two well-known verses of the Vulgate Psalter: *Eructavit cor meum verbum bonum* (Ps. 45:1: "My heart belches out the good word") and *Memoriam*

abundantiae suavitatis tuae eructabunt (Ps. 144:15: "They will
belch out the memory of the abundance of your sweetness"). Here
are his own words:

> The words of the prophet do not apply to everyone. He said,
> "They will belch out the memory of your sweetness," and
> not everyone is nourished by such a memory. It is obvious
> that someone who has not tasted and those who have done
> no more than taste will not belch. A belch comes forth from
> a certain fullness and satiety.[132]

The point he is making is a very practical one. A common
reason why people often find themselves blocked in prayer is
that they have abandoned or greatly diminished the practice of
lectio divina. In the words of Psalm 102:5, "They forgot to eat
their bread." Prayer is our faith-filled response to God's self-
revelation. As the radiance of revelation fades in our hearts we
are less willing and able to respond fervently. Our prayer is fueled
by our faith, which, in turn, is initiated and sustained by God's
self-revelation. When faith becomes stale, prayer dries up. This is
why regular personal contact with the Scriptures is so important.
It is not only that we need to learn more about God. We need
to discover more about ourselves by looking into the scriptural
mirror.

It is from the Scriptures that we learn the good news of
God's deep, abiding, unconditional, and personal love. Unless
we have embraced the image of God as an all-loving Father we
will probably never experience the inclination to spend time in
personal prayer. Of course, when we are desperate, we will resort
to anything that might help extricate us from imminent danger,
but this is not the same as deliberately putting aside alternative
activities to dedicate our energies to pursuing personal communion with God. Familiarity with the Scriptures slowly reveals to

us the loving face of God, correcting mistaken notions that might cause us to hold back.

As Saint Augustine frequently reminds us, God draws us by way of delight. It is true that feelings of devotion are not the whole sum of the spiritual life, but they are not nothing. Long periods of emotional aridity are common concomitants to progress in prayer, but they are almost always interrupted by what Saint Gregory the Great termed "breathing spaces" (*respiria*), in which a momentary glimpse of what is beyond our normal experience captivates our attention and gives us the courage to continue our journey of prayer. There is a lot of energy in these brief experiences. On the other hand, long periods of totally unrelieved dryness are more often a signal that we have drifted away from lectio divina or, alternatively, that there are components of our behavior that are seriously inconsistent with gospel living. Most often, however, our aridity is due to a neglect of affective reading of Scripture. We are experiencing the effects of a famine of the word, and the quality of our spiritual life is beginning to deteriorate.

Most of us have experienced the power of the Scriptures to add a sparkle to our commitment to Christian values, but it can easily happen that we allow ourselves to be drawn in alternative directions and either give less time to our reading of the Bible or do so with less attention. It may be that lectio divina needs to be approached on the understanding that "the medium is the message." What is important is that we approach the Word with meekness, humility, and docility, ready to be formed by it. We are sending the message that we are at God's disposition. With such an attitude, we will know what God intends us to hear by the impact a text makes on us. If God is silent then, perhaps, that may convey the message that we are not really listening.

At some stage in our life it would be worthwhile to spend time pondering Psalm 119. Almost every verse of this long poem is a celebration of God's great gift of the Torah. It becomes clear as we pass from one verse to the next that the "law" of which the Psalm speaks is more than a set of regulations. It is teaching; its function is the formation of God's people. It is a record of the wonderful things God has done in creation, in the redemption of the people, and in showing forth to all who would pay attention the glory of the divine Name. It is revelation. In addition to its obvious meaning we can, perhaps, apply each mention of the "law" to our own personal revelation when, in the experience of faith or vocation, we believe that God has spoken to us. It is when we meditate on what God has done and who God is that praise is born in our hearts and with it a trustful hope that will fire into flame whenever life becomes difficult. All true prayer is a response to God's self-revelation.

Loving Father,

In various ways and at different times you have spoken to us.

In these last times you have revealed yourself most fully
In your Son, Jesus Christ.

May we receive this revelation with meek and humble hearts

And so come to learn of your great love for us.
We ask this through Christ our Lord. Amen!

CHAPTER TWELVE

The Grace of Leisure

I n our busy world leisure is often understood as the opposite to work.[133] It is regarded as downtime when we can do what we like. In many cases this involves activity as frantic and frenetic as what happens during work, with the result that we can be more exhausted by leisure than by engaging in our usual occupation. In such situations, it is not a question of finding ourselves but of losing ourselves in a variety of activities that engage, stimulate, and excite us. Even in Latin there is confusion in the understanding of *otium*. Does it mean "leisure" or "idleness"? Among the Latin fathers of the Church it more often has a negative connotation since they, like us, found it is easier to condemn abuses than to make a case for what is healthy and nourishing of the self. So it is important that we make distinctions and attempt to clarify what this misunderstood term signifies. Fundamentally I understand leisure, as it is used in the monastic tradition to mean a time and space of freedom and recuperation, in which the deep self can find fuller expression and, eventually, reach its perfection.[134]

In a paradoxical sense, self-realization is the goal and principal task of the spiritual journey. As we have explained, this is not an invitation to narcissism, but is an act of obedience to God's call embedded in our nature. We were not designed to be incomplete beings, full of unfulfilled yearnings and unrealized potentialities. We were made to be alive with the life of God. To aspire to anything less is to sell ourselves short. And while we will attain this perfection only in eternal life, we can yet have moments in which we catch glimpses of what it will be like to be fully free from external constraints and allowed to be simply ourselves.

In 1990 Mihaly Csikszentmihalyi published his book *Flow: The Psychology of Optimal Experience,* introducing a new term into the language.[135] The optimal experiences about which he wrote were moments in which persons are substantially free of outside pressure and able to concentrate fully on what they are doing.[136] Whatever the task may be, whether it is art, writing, music, sport, or science, it is just within the range of their capabilities so that they have the necessary skills to perform it but, at the same time, they are challenged to extend their limits. This means that close concentration is necessary, not in a way that brings them anxiety but because they find in such close application a sense of delight. So close is the identification of the doer and the deed that it is almost as though the activity performs itself. It flows. In such a state of consciousness distractions are easily banished so that the person is fully immersed in the action. Meanwhile, there is some process of internal feedback that communicates a sense that everything is going well. An experienced archer may know that the arrow is on course even before it reaches the target—because it feels right. When a person acts in a state of flow, the activity is usually of a high standard, objectively speaking. Subjectively it is the source of happiness, creativity, satisfaction, fulfillment. Often enough success does not lead to pride or arrogance, because the person feels that what was done was performed under the influence of something larger than themselves, before which they can feel only humility. Writers sometimes gratefully attribute their work to their muse inspiring them as they wrote. The work itself, as well as its aftermath, is relatively free of egoistic demands. To some extent it is autonomous; it stands apart from the ordinary demands of everyday life.

The state of flow is usually reserved to those with a certain clarity about the goals in their lives that shapes their motivation so that what they do under this impulsion is self-motivating, or autotelic. This clarity enables them to exercise a high degree of self-control in the conduct of their lives. They keep expanding their universe in an ordered and systematic way, developing their skills and resisting the ever-present temptation to dissipate their energies on things that do not matter. They are practitioners of leisure, not of idleness. We may think of someone like Mozart as one who was naturally gifted and did not have to do much to display his dazzling talents. He himself would probably not agree with this since we know he was critical of the following generation for dissipating their energies and wasting their time. Even huge talent requires nurturing and hard work.

The concept of flow can help us to understand the true nature of leisure. Far from being an excuse for dissipation, authentic leisure enables us to find ourselves. It requires us to be somewhat free from external constraints, but this freedom is more a state of mind rather than the quality of the task and certainly more than the mere cessation of alienating obligations. For me shaving is a burden; I do it only because it is expected of me, and I avoid it if I can. For some men, however, it is a moment of leisure. Concentrating on their task they happily apply their whole energies to slaughtering every hapless hair that pokes its head above the surface, dispelling for the moment all the cares and anxieties that bedevil the rest of their day. The difference between leisure and nonleisure is, to some extent, subjective. If I give myself entirely to the task at hand, engaging my skills and putting my heart in what I am doing, it may not matter much what the work is. Whatever it is, I will come away refreshed and happy and the task itself will probably be better done. Sometimes we read about the saints that they gave themselves fully to whatever they were doing, no matter how humble or humdrum. This is not some deliberate choice imposed by an unbending will.

It is more likely the natural overflow of a heart that is undivided, that simply lives each moment and performs each task as though nothing else in the world mattered.

Leisure has been a cherished value in monastic culture wherever there are communities that are not defined by the work they do, that exist primarily to facilitate the spiritual growth of those who are admitted to them. Fully functional families find it both useful and delightful to make provision both for quality time to spend together and for time alone to pursue personal interests. People are so different, and their needs are not the same. They are not formed only by common tasks to be accomplished, but they also need to be encouraged to grow to the limit of their particular possibilities both in what is assigned to them and in what they themselves choose.

Monastic communities, like families, have to engage in work that provides sufficiently to support a modest lifestyle. They have to be alert to the possibility that work will expand to exclude other activities that have as their main purpose the enriching of the lives of the members. There is more to life than moneymaking. Activities play an important role in the development of individuals and in building up a common culture. Insofar as there is the possibility of choice, the range of activities embraced, encouraged, or allowed should grow out of the possibilities presented by gifts and talents of each. Such occupations offer the possibility of self-expression and ultimately will be found to be fulfilling and character-forming.

The fact that the subjective quality of the work enhances the quality of what is produced is demonstrated by the esteem in which the fruit of monastic labor is held. Marketing of monastic products often takes the line that there is something special present because of those involved in the production. The monastery is not a sweatshop; the work of monastics is not the fruit of mindless toil, but is seen as benefiting from the pursuit of excellence that is typical of those who embrace the monastic way.[137]

Leisure is purposeful and personal activity that aspires to be marked by flow. It is not slackness or idleness or the pursuit of recreational activities. It is, above all, being attentive to the present moment, open to all its implications, living it to the full. This implies a certain looseness in lifestyle that allows heart and mind to drift away from time to time. It is a mistake to think that the good life is merely a matter of shoehorning the maximum number of good works into a day. It is more important to do a few things well, being present to the tasks undertaken, and leaving room for recuperation and reflection. It is the opposite of being enslaved by the past or postponing commitment by dreaming about an ideal future. Leisure means being free from anything that would impede, color, or subvert the perception of and participation in reality. Far from being the headlong pursuit of escapist activities and having fun, authentic leisure is a very serious matter because it is the product of an attentive and listening attitude to life. It is a matter of concentration, and concentration always involves narrowing the range of attention by eliminating everything that would dissipate the sharp focus. This is how Josef Pieper expressed this truth in his classical essay on leisure:

> Leisure is a form of silence which is the prerequisite of the apprehension of reality. Leisure is a receptive attitude of mind, a contemplative attitude, and it is not only the occasion but also the capacity for steeping oneself in the whole of creation.[138]

Anyone who has tried to have a serious conversation with someone who is totally engaged with what may be happening on their cellphone knows something of the inability of human consciousness to be in two places at once. We can pretend to be paying attention, but in reality we do not succeed. On the other hand, we always enjoy being with persons who give us their total attention for the time when they are with us. This was my impression in speaking briefly with Mother Teresa of Calcutta; for a brief moment nobody else in the world existed for her.[139] When we concentrate on one thing our attention is undivided. Most people overestimate their capacity for multitasking, and as a result the results they produce are shoddy. More significant, perhaps, is that persons feel somewhat detached from the several tasks they are performing. The outcome is that they are less effective in imprinting their own character on the work done. For them the finishing of the task is important; no attention is paid to its quality, and as a result excellence is rarely achieved.

The freedom to be attentive requires, paradoxically, that we renounce the desire to control what happens around us, to manipulate reality, to impose our will on events or on other people. We need to respect the alterity of the world around us and of other people; to allow them to be themselves and not to attempt to make them conform to our expectations or demands. We may think that those who try to keep control of everything around them are strong and dominating people, attempting to rule others and to mold them in their own imperial likeness. Usually this is not so. Control freaks are most often fearful people who are threatened by the prospect that events would be allowed to take an independent direction. Underneath the firm grip and the bluster is a wavering self-confidence that fears to face the unexpected. By constraining everything to squeeze itself into the hard shell of their expectations, they fail to read and respect the reality of the world around them. They are heedless of what is outside themselves because they are driven mercilessly by their own insecurity. Their life is a constant battle to prevent reality from asserting its independence. Their inner voices are secretly shouting so loudly that they can hear nothing else.

To experience the relaxed freedom that belongs to the essence of authentic leisure we need to learn to appreciate silence, not only as an absence of outward noise and clamor, but also as an inner stillness that is the hallmark of an undivided heart. Such inward quiet is a little like soundproofing. It not only does not create noise but it somehow absorbs the noise that comes from outside itself and neutralizes its power to disturb. A person who is so intent on a task that time seems to fade away can often keep doing the task even when surrounded by a maelstrom of potential disturbances. As we often say, "Time passes quickly when you are having fun." When our work engages us, we do not notice the minutes or hours as they slip past.

Some harmony has to be achieved between our search for an ambience that allows us to be fully ourselves and the work demanded of us by the particular situation in which we live. Living on a deserted island may be fine to dream about, but should we emigrate we would soon find that our days were filled with making provision for our survival. The benefit of living among people is that these necessary tasks are shared among many, and we need do no more than our proportion of them to satisfy our basic needs. The downside of this is that we may be obliged to do things with which otherwise we would not bother. Such unchosen work is, for many people, a burden that makes their life less frolicsome. Even though their involvement in their allocated tasks is reasonable and fair, they may begin to see it as a form of servitude. Their attitude makes the work heavier because it erodes any satisfaction they might have in doing the job well.

Even while many people dislike their work, or dislike having to work, the work itself produces benefits for them, especially pecuniary benefits. This creates a dilemma. Work provides them with the money they need not only to procure the necessities of life but also to acquire some of its luxuries. The more they work, the more money they earn, the more possible it is for them to render the time not spent working in ways that are meaningful and pleasurable. Working more diminishes their free time, but it allows

them to shape that free time in ways that correspond most closely
to their personal aspirations. Often enough this means filling their
free time with gratifying activities, so that it is no longer, strictly
speaking, "free time" but time spent on meeting the aspirational
needs induced in them by the organs of social communication.
These may well involve persons "losing themselves" rather than
"finding themselves." Obviously, some effort is needed to arrive
at a life-giving balance between what used to be termed "servile
work" and activities that are recuperative, relaxing, and creative.

True leisure demands a measure of solitude and silence to
allow the deep self to emerge from its chrysalis. This can be hard
to find in a world that cherishes communication and involvement.
Uninterrupted solitude can be interpreted as antisocial, and the
slightest delay in responding to text messages and emails can be
regarded as discourteous, or even indicative of a disaster having
occurred. Solitariness itself is not leisure, but it is the matrix
upon which leisure grows. But there is no guarantee that this will
happen, or happen quickly. I was impressed by the honesty of the
novelist Don De Lillo in describing the way wasting time contributes to the process of writing.

> A writer takes earnest measures to secure his solitude and
> then finds endless ways to squander it. . . . But the work
> itself, you know—sentence by sentence, page by page—it's
> much too intimate, much too private, to come from any-
> where but deep within the writer himself. It comes out of
> all the time a writer wastes. We stand around, look out the
> window, walk down the hall, come back to the page, and, in
> those intervals, something subterranean is forming, a literal
> dream that comes out of day-dreaming. It's too deep to be
> attributed to clear sources.[140]

The flow necessary for truly creative work is not the same thing as merely wasting time, but for flow to happen there must be a willingness to spend time disengaging from workaday activities and slowly opening oneself to a different conscious horizon. Sometimes it seems like panning for gold. For much of the time there is only silt in the pan, but eventually, if one has chosen the location right, the glimmer of gold will stand out from the dross. Stepping back from the usual round of activities liberates consciousness from its shackles and paves the way for pleasant surprise. It is probably no accident that Archimedes was relaxing in the bath when his eureka moment hit him.

It is hard to structure leisure into our lives because all sorts of other activities crowd in to exploit the emptiness we have worked so hard to create. Thomas Merton was aware of this challenge:

> The contemplative life must provide an area, a space of liberty, of silence, in which possibilities are allowed to surface and new choices—beyond routine choices—become manifest. It should create a new experience of time, not as a stopgap, stillness, but as *temps vierge*—not as a blank to be filled or an untouched space to be conquered and violated, but a space which can enjoy its own potentialities and hopes—and its own presence to itself. One's *own* time. But not dominated by one's own ego and its demands. Hence open to others—compassionate time, rooted in the sense of common illusion and in criticism of it.[141]

Fruitful leisure starts life as empty space. We find it hard to make room for nothing in our crowded lives; like nature we abhor a vacuum. We usually prefer to do something ostensibly useful. A period of involuntary inactivity due to unforeseen circumstances we find very hard to endure. Look at people in a queue, or in a doctor's waiting room, or in the departure lounge of a delayed flight. We fret because our projected sequence of events has been interrupted and we are left hanging. Even when we plan leisure we sometimes do not feel right because nothing is happening. Leisure shares with silence its unproductive character, but its uselessness is sweet. As Max Picard wrote:

> Silence, however, stands outside the world of profit and utility; it cannot be exploited for profit; you cannot get anything out of it. It is "unproductive." Therefore it is regarded as valueless. Yet there is more help and healing in silence than in all the "useful things." Purposeless, unexploitable silence suddenly appears at the side of the all-too-purposeful, and frightens us by its very purposelessness. It interferes with the regular flow of the purposeful. It strengthens the untouchable, it lessens the damage inflicted by exploitation. It makes things whole again, by taking them back from the world of dissipation into the world of wholeness. It gives something of its own holy uselessness, for that is what silence itself is: holy uselessness.[142]

Leisure means living gently; it is the opposite of being driven or obsessed. It involves getting on with the job in hand and detaching oneself from it when it is time to move on to something else. To some extent leisure invites us to cultivate the virtue of inefficiency, or at least be less obsessed with efficiency, as Pope Francis seems to have recommended.[143] We are far more likely to notice the scenery if we dawdle along the way than if we rocket along at mind-numbing speed. Leisure calls us to avoid the cumulative sense of incompletion that occurs when we find ourselves burdened with the weight of so many cares and unfinished tasks. It is a childlike concern only for the present. I suppose it was easier in a world not dominated by calendars and clocks simply to take each day as it comes. On the other hand, making the effort to overthrow the tyranny of time yields proportionately higher profits to those of us who try it sometimes. It is like a liberation. We have to realize, however, that the tyrant is inside us, not outside.

Leisure is fragile; it needs to be defended; there are too many things that can displace it or so modify it that it loses its particular character. A group that really tries to give its members room to breathe is a blessing. Time and space are, of their very nature, quantifiable and therefore limited. The gift of time is a very precious one: time for oneself, time for one another, time to listen, encourage, and support, time to step back and discern, to assess the quality of actions, time to develop culture and ritual and good liturgy. Space for people to grow, space for different gifts, space for the stranger, space to pass through crises. Leisure is, as Pope John Paul II often insisted, about building a culture of humanization.

Any group that takes seriously the advantages of providing for its members an appropriate measure of free time will stand out clearly in our purpose-driven world. The aim of a disciplined asceticism is not to restrict the amount of free time available but to ensure that it is creatively used. It is important, therefore, to safeguard the integrity of each so that leisure is both true to self and harmonious within the communal setting.

Leisure is one of the effects of a way of life that has at its heart the promotion of a fully human existence. It deliberately moderates the inflow of external demands so that what is interior and personal is not swamped. This is a noble concern, but it is not so easy to implement. We soon discover that the possibilities of escape from fully personal living are both legion and attractive, and that it requires persevering effort to maintain mindfulness in a world that constantly summons us to distraction.

We are all familiar with persons who work too hard, who are obsessive, ambitious, or hyper-diligent, who take on too many jobs and never seem to reach a point when they are not preoccupied with what has to be done next. Such people experience little leisure.

Other strangers to leisure are less visible. These are the slothful, those who lack commitment, those who seek means to insulate themselves from the demands of the present moment and, if possible, to escape from them. Such activities as they consent to do expand to fill all available time so that there is never any possibility of undertaking anything unexpected or for the service of others. To the casual observer it may appear that the lazy person leads a more leisured life, but in reality such a vacuous existence falls far short of the true meaning of leisure because their hearts and minds are full of emptiness and there is no room for anything more.

It is worth remembering the Old Testament notion of Sabbath. One day in seven was designated as a day on which no work was to be done, a day of rest but also a day of celebration. It is perhaps interesting that one of the four practical means suggested by Thomas Merton toward recovering the contemplative dimension of life was, precisely, a renewed observance of Sunday, not in the puritanical banishment of work, nor as a chance for recreation, but as a feast for the spirit. What he says of Sunday captures something of the essence of authentic leisure.

Sunday is a day of contemplation not because it is a day without work, a day when the shops and banks and offices are closed. [*Sic!*] But because it is sacred to the mystery of the resurrection. Sunday is the "Lord's Day" not in the sense that, on one day out of the week, one must stop and think of Him, but because it breaks into the ceaseless, "secular" round of time with a burst of light out of a sacred eternity. We stop working and rushing about on Sunday not only in order to rest up and start over on Monday, but in order to collect our wits and realize the relative meaninglessness of the secular business which fills the other six days of the week, and taste the satisfaction of a peace which surpasses understanding and which is given us by Christ. Sunday reminds us of the peace that should filter through the whole week when our work is properly oriented.[144]

The Sabbath is a time of celebration; it should include a global acceptance of reality as the gift of God's loving providence. To be fully alive generates in us a positive attitude to everything, just as being only half alive tends to make us critical and dismissive. We are all bound by the universal law of labor, but as far as we can, we ought to make provision for space in which other possibilities can be glimpsed, desires enkindled, and energies generated to make of our world a better place.

The ancient Greeks used to speak of play as a virtue: *eutrapelia*.[145] It would be wrong to make of leisure something that is deadly serious, a heavy burden on those who would prefer to be occupied in something useful. There is a certain lightness about leisure, a playfulness, if you will, that makes time thus spent delightful and energizing. To have no leisure is the lot of the slave; willfully to eliminate or restrict leisure is to inhibit our powers of creativity and ultimately to stand in the way of God's plan for his creation.

Lord God, Creator and sustainer of all things,
You created us in your own image
To grow in likeness to you, to be ever more creative,
And to use our talents to advance your kingdom
Of righteousness, peace, and joy in the Holy Spirit.
Keep us faithful to this calling
So that in all we do you may be glorified.
We ask this through Christ, our Lord. Amen!

CHAPTER THIRTEEN

The Grace of
Silence

ollowing our reflections on the topic of leisure there may
be some advantage in speaking more explicitly about the
role played by solitude and silence in our coming to wisdom.[146] Fundamentally the matter is simple. We cannot think
deeply and speak at the same time, so unless we shut up sometimes, we are never going to attain much in the way of profundity. And because deeper thinking is required if we are to explore
the spiritual world, an unreflective spiritual life is scarcely worth
having. An appreciation of silence and solitude will help us to
free ourselves from the constraints the secular world imposes
on us. Alfred North Whitehead wrote in his book *Religion in
the Making*: "Religion is what a man does with his own solitude.
And if you are never solitary you are never religious."[147] I do not
think that he is referring here to institutional silence and solitude
such as that about which monastic rules speak. There is question,
rather, of a certain quietness of mind and mouth that comes from
deep within us, if we allow it the opportunity. Something happens when we are reflective and quiet. We have the chance to be
still and know that God is God. In the contemporary world, there
is a danger that our spirituality will follow the expectations of
ambient culture and become too extroverted, pursuing external
good works with palpable zeal, but without much attention paid
to interior components of virtuous living. If you have read Susan

Cain's book *Quiet: The Power of Introverts in a World that Can't Stop Talking*,[148] you will be aware of how much Western society contributes to such an outcome.

We live in a world in which communication is highly valued and its absence seems like an indicator of our little worth. It is as though the various means of communication are elements in our life-support system. Have you ever noticed how your fellow passengers reach for their cellphones as a newly landed plane begins to taxi toward the terminal? When the screen lights up, so do their faces in anticipation. If there are messages for them, all is well; if not, they dolefully return the phone to its place as though it has let them down. It is as if we cease to exist unless someone is calling us or contacting us. We are held in existence like a spider in its web, supported by our network of contacts. If this fragile support system breaks, we fall to the ground. The content of the communication seems to matter less than the fact that somebody out there acknowledges our existence and wishes to link up with us.

Granted the importance of communication and the anxiety we experience in its absence, why is silence regarded as such an important element in leading a serious spiritual life? This is true not only for introverts, for whom quiet time is a chance for recuperation and replenishment, but also for those on the opposite end of the scale, whose sense of well-being depends on talking and engaging with other people. Perhaps extroverts need to work harder to ensure that they do not neglect to maintain and grow their inner resources.

In the first place, we have to remember the blunt warning in the book of Proverbs: "In much speaking you will not avoid sinning" (Prov. 10:19). It is a common observation that religious people express their resistance to God and their detachment from their neighbor less by overt actions than by thoughts and in their conversation. It is almost as though the evil within them, that they are trying to suppress by being "good," somehow escapes despite their best efforts. Saint James devotes the third chapter of his epistle to this theme and concludes that those who have reached the point of being able to control their tongues are already perfect. It is worthwhile recalling this passage.

> Not many of you should become teachers, my brothers, knowing that we will receive a greater judgment. We all are deficient in many ways. Anyone who is never at fault in speaking is a perfect man, restraining his whole body. If we put bits into the mouths of horses so that they obey us, we can direct the whole body. Consider ships. They are large and are driven by strong winds, but they are directed by a very small rudder wherever the pilot wills. Similarly, the tongue is a small member, but it makes great boasts. Consider what a great forest is set on fire by a small spark. The tongue also is a fire, a world of lawlessness among the members. It defiles the whole body, sets alight the course of his life, and is itself set alight by hell. All kinds of beasts, birds, reptiles, and creatures of the sea are tamed and have been tamed by humans, but no one can tame the tongue. It is an ever-active evil, full of lethal poison. With it we praise our Lord and Father, and with it we curse people, who have been made in God's likeness. Out of the same mouth come blessing and cursing. My brothers, this should not be. Can both freshwater and saltwater flow out from the same source? My brothers, can a fig tree bear olives, or a grapevine bear figs? Neither can a salt spring produce fresh water. (Jas. 3:1–10)

A text like this reminds us that although we are fairly careful about our actions we are often slack about our words, especially those spoken in situations where we do not have to keep up a public facade of goodness. It is sometimes remarked that the private conversations of priests and religious workers when they consider themselves "off duty" are not always edifying. To say the least! The more we have to exert ourselves to behave in public, the more tempted we are to break out from our constraints when we are off-screen. Remember the expletive-laden conversations in Nixon's White House. Yes, upright behavior is what others expect of us and what we ourselves desire, but we need also to consider the source from which our actions flow. It is not enough to put on an act that fools some of the people some of the time. Good actions need to issue from a pure heart. If the source is polluted, then everything that flows from it will be somehow contaminated, no matter how good it may seem on the surface. When we are under pressure to live at a level that is higher than our natural status, there is a tendency for us to compensate for having to be publicly good by privately venting the negativity that is within us.

Not all of us recognize that there is continuity between what we think and say, and what we do. If we spend a lot of time thinking and speaking about sexual immorality, for example, it is likely that progressively our values will be eroded so that misconduct becomes less unthinkable. The same holds with the practice of charity. If we are judgmental and condemnatory in our thoughts, these negative feelings will eventually come to the surface in our words, and will soon find expression in our actions. And this even though we may take care that our malice is concealed from others, and perhaps from ourselves.

"From the abundance of the heart the mouth speaks" (Lk. 6:45), whether we intend it or not. Every message comes packaged with a meta-message, every text has a subtext; even the most banal statement often comes with a spin. Weasel words enable us to make a spiteful point without seeming to; thanks to their hidden content we can stab someone in the back and remain blameless. When we bad-mouth somebody, what we are really doing is suggesting that we are superior to that person. If I say that Pablo Casals's cello technique was defective, I am really planting the idea that I am a better cellist than he—or, I would be, if only I knew how to play the cello! Saying anything negative about anyone implies that I am better than they are. "Stalin was a monster" means "I am a better man than he." I would not have to insist on it if I were not secretly unsure whether I really am much better. Detraction comes from insecurity. When I walk past the cat I do not feel compelled to prove that my knowledge of medieval history is better than hers; others may doubt it, but I am completely confident that it is. I do not go around boasting about it or criticizing the cat's ignorance. When I speak badly about others it is often a matter of compensating for the bad things said about me—not by others, in fact, but by myself, especially by some form of internalized parental voice that is always scolding me. It is when I am insecure concerning aspects of myself that I begin to harp on the defects of others. If I take care to listen to my criticisms of others I will learn a lot about my own liabilities.

A sustained effort to monitor our speech is a good indication that we are serious about the spiritual life and that we have begun to live by some form of personal discipline. A refusal to be complicit in gossip, detraction, and slander is likely to change for the better the quality of our interaction with others and improve our peace of heart. It is not only a matter of watching our own speech; we must also limit our listening to aimless chatter. We need to learn the art of gently diverting or cutting short any conversation that is beginning to focus on the faults of parties not present. The laborious struggle to exercise discipline in this matter may also lead us in the direction of useful self-scrutiny. Why do we feel the need to talk so much? Why is it so hard to stop bad-mouthing others? Why are we so lacking in compassion that we are constantly harping on deficiencies? Why are we so happy to listen to criticism of others? Submitting our speech to discipline will require much effort, and the struggle to do so will endure for most of our life. If we sin often by speaking, then we will sin less often by speaking less.

Speaking less invites us to give more attention to the inner world, the world of spirit. To take a step back from the effects of social conditioning and to think our own thoughts for a while. To listen for the promptings of our conscience, perhaps pointing us in the direction of a more life-giving path. To be alert to the still, small voice of the Holy Spirit's interior guidance. We will sometimes find that prayer comes more easily because we are less distracted by extraneous sounds.

In addition to watching what we say, an effort to reduce the physical noise around us can lead to a greater reflectiveness. Sometimes resisting the impulse to turn on the radio or television as a background to whatever else we are doing may be a beginning. In an effort to facilitate the contemplative life, monasteries are typically built in areas that are somewhat remote from the bustle of city life or, at least, are large enough to surround themselves with a buffer zone of gardens and trees. Within the monastic environment, there is a conscious effort to do things with a minimum of noise. We can learn from this that there is something to be said for living in a softer, gentler ambience.

People visiting a monastery are often surprised by the quiet: they can hear the birds singing or the rustle of the trees in the wind. Some are delighted, but others are disoriented, so accustomed are they to a constant background of noise: traffic, machinery, television, conversation. It can happen that silence becomes uncomfortable and even frightening. That is why we avoid it. It can happen that when we are quiet, the inner voices that are kept at bay by noise and activity begin to speak, and what they have to say to us is not always welcome. Sometimes we discover within ourselves tendencies and desires that run contrary to the chosen direction of our life. In the same way, silence reveals to us what has yet to be done if our spiritual life is to be real. This was noticed in a reality television program in which laymen were induced to live in a monastery for an extended period. One of the participants exploring his immersion in the monastic ambience remarked, "What's happening in the silence is that stuff is coming up that I normally don't give attention to and I can get ambushed."

The ancient monks went out into the desert to engage in spiritual warfare. Their experience was that where there is no distraction, it is impossible to avoid or postpone the inevitable clash with the negative elements in our own nature and history. This battle is inevitable; it can be postponed, but it cannot be avoided. Without a good measure of silence we will be merely skimming the surface of the spiritual life, doing good deeds and practicing the virtues, without ever scrutinizing the motives and intentions that inspire them. And, from time to time, we will be shocked when we behave in a way that is inconsistent with our ideals. We will be puzzled why this should be so. Our conclusion must be that a quiet and unexciting ambience is a valuable adjunct to our efforts to live spiritually. And if we cannot live thus always, there is an advantage in seeking to withdraw occasionally from the noise and bustle of ordinary life into a zone of silence in which we can add depth to the spiritual pursuit.

However much silence is an ideal for those professing to live a contemplative life, the fact remains that the observance of silence is a perpetual issue in coenobitic monasteries. This is because, due to the practical demands of interaction and cooperation, it can never be absolute. For this reason, the notional boundaries between silence and acceptable speech are always being breached. This happens despite a historic abundance of legislation and exhortation. I once met a distinguished abbot of our order on his way to conduct several regular visitations. I asked him over lunch if he found it hard to keep the different situations of each community separate in his mind. He replied in the negative, saying that he usually wrote the visitation reports before he left home so that he just had to tweak them a little when he arrived on the spot. He said, "You can always say something like, 'Silence leaves much to be desired' and give a little homily on silence and that works in most communities." If the value of silence is not always practically affirmed even in monasteries, it is likely that its utility is even less appreciated outside the monastic enclosure.

Monastic legislators have spent a lot of energy speaking about silence, probably because rules governing this practice have been honored mainly in their breach. It has to be remembered that many of these texts derive from an oral/aural culture in which most people would have had an instinctive preference for verbal communication over reading from books. To make provision for substantial and ongoing contact with the beliefs and values that undergird spiritual living, times for reading and reflection had to be protected.

Saint Bernard of Clairvaux, although he recognized the value of good speech in building up a supportive community, also knew that Christian and monastic values can be undermined by undisciplined talking. He wrote about speech that is characterized by dissipation, indecency, boasting, trickery, detraction.[149] He did not allow coarse jokes, detraction, words of boasting, and impatience.[150] He condemned words that are foolish, empty, lying, idle, misleading, abusive, indecent, self-excusatory.[151] Supposing that twelfth-century Clairvaux under Saint Bernard was near the top of the league tables in monastic observance, it is encouraging to the rest of us that even in such a supportive environment fruitful silence remains more of an ideal than a reality.

An enthusiasm for news and information of various kinds provides us with the content of many frivolous conversations. We call it "small talk" even though it can consume a large amount of time and, beyond that, can lead to the kind of aimless gossip that easily spills over from the merely entertaining to the subtly malicious. Our participation in such sessions is often the result of our inability to concentrate on what we are doing, and the consequent tendency to keep our eyes peeled for anything unusual or worthy of further comment. Those who do their own work and mind their own business will have little to contribute to the daily roundup of newsworthy events. For Bernard of Clairvaux, this aimless curiosity is an early stage of a process that develops into serious spiritual decline.[152] "Let none of you, brothers, underestimate the time that is consumed in useless words. After long periods of small talk [*post longas confabulationes*[the mind is found to be, as it were, empty; meditation is less marked by devotion, feeling is dry and the holocaust of prayer less rich [*pinguis*]."[153]

The potential harm that attaches to the undisciplined tongue should not discourage us from trying to upgrade the quality of our conversation. When our speech is under discipline it is far more likely to be encouraging and instructive to others, less prone to sowing the seeds of dissension and more effective as a vehicle for transmitting the wisdom slowly acquired through long experience. Above all, such interior silence that expresses itself through outward attentiveness makes a person a ready listener, able not only to hear what is said but also to perceive what is meant and to have some appreciation of the inner state of the one who speaks. And sometimes to hear what is not being expressed explicitly. To arrive at such a state requires much self-restraint and a sincere concern to listen to others sympathetically. To welcome what other people have to say is to offer a rare form of hospitality. Good listening is the sincerest form of kindness and the supreme mark of honor that we can give another.

The other person is not the only beneficiary, as we know from our own experience. If we set ourselves the task of really listening we will often hear a word that touches us powerfully, whether as a comfort or a challenge. Nothing is more certain than the fact that God speaks to us through human agencies, but in a very subtle way. Unless we listen carefully we may miss the message. When faithful Christians engage in mutual listening, Christ is present. Who knows what blessings will result?

The only way to be blameless in speech is to be blameless in thought. First we have to set our heart on the ultimate goal in such a way that our thoughts swing back in that direction by the force of gravity, like a pendulum. Until we reach that point we need to exercise discipline over what comes out of our mouth. Saint Bernard thinks that it is a good exercise of self-restraint to undertake during Lent.

> [During Lent] let the ear fast from its evil itch to listen to stories and rumors and whatever is unprofitable or has little bearing on salvation. Let the tongue fast from detraction and grumbling, from useless, vain, and scurrilous words, and—because of the seriousness of silence—sometimes even from words that could be necessary.[154]

In the seventh chapter of his Rule, Saint Benedict gives us some idea of how he believes a monk should speak. The monk's speech should be gentle, without laughter, humble, serious, not excessive, reasonable, not loud.[155] This is to put a limit on self-certain self-assertion, and to express one's views in a way that freely permits the other to differ. To speak in the subjunctive mood, as the English sociologist Richard Sennett terms such speech, is to pepper one's discourse with such expressions as "perhaps," "maybe," or "I wonder whether there is not another way of looking at the matter."[156] In Saint Benedict's view, as a monk makes spiritual progress, so his speech gradually assumes some of these characteristics. As with the rest of the chapter on humility, the steps on the ladder are not so much good things to be pursued or put into practice as manifestations or indications that progress is being made. They are the consequences of truthful living, of living in an ongoing attitude of truth before God, before one's neighbor, and before self.

We should not be too severe in the matter of silence. Saint Bernard recognized the importance of sociability in a monastic community as a means of acquiring love. Here we must reassert the principles of moderation and reasonableness: light conversation has value. It can act as a lubricant in interpersonal relations. Although the topic under discussion may have no lasting significance, the fact that it is being discussed amicably builds up a sense of solidarity and friendship in the community. Casual conversation is an important though undramatic means of achieving reconciliation. As Churchill is erroneously credited with saying, "Jaw-jaw is better than war-war." The content of the exchange is less important than the fact that those who have previously kept themselves at a distance are coming together. Often enough, it is by laying a foundation of trivial conversation over months or years that it becomes possible for serious and life-enhancing discussions to follow.

In a sense, the degree to which the whole spiritual pursuit has advanced is often signified by the manner in which people express themselves. Being able to participate in serious conversation without the unconscious need to dominate proceedings is a fair indication that persons have made solid progress in bringing to heel the various unconscious forces that roil within them. The whole program of Christian asceticism is paralleled by progressive improvement in meaningful conversation.

The Christian Church is best understood as a schooling in conversation. Such a schooling is necessary because truthful converse requires the recognition that the "self" who speaks must first be heard by others in order to be a self at all. It requires that I recognise others as themselves constitutive of my own identity. To be a self requires a mutuality of trust that permits the risk of recognising my inescapable interdependence on others. In order to find myself I must dispossess myself.[157]

Much to the puzzlement of modern readers the ancient monastic tradition concerning silence has been particularly adamant in its prohibition of laughter. Saint Benedict subjected laughter to eternal banishment, *aeterna clausura*, probably without notable success. Oddly enough, Saint Aelred regards laughter as an anticipation of the joys of heaven and not wholly to be banished. This is how Aelred expresses himself.

> "Isaac" is interpreted as "laughter" and signifies that about which the Lord spoke in the Gospel, "Blessed are you who mourn now; you shall laugh" (Lk. 6:21). This laughter does not mean scurrility and coarse jokes, but a certain unspeakable joy that we will have [when we are] with God. Of the joy we ought to have some part in this life. We ought to rejoice in that hope that we must have in God and in those promises which God has promised us.[158]

Surprisingly, Karl Rahner writes in the same vein: "The laughter of daily life announces and shows that one is on good terms with reality." Here is his full text:

> But you shall laugh. Thus it is written. And because God's Word also had recourse to human words in order to express what shall one day be when all shall have been— that is why a mystery of eternity also lies deeply hidden, but real, in everyday life; that is why the laughter of daily life announces and shows that one is on good terms with reality, even in advance of that all-powerful and eternal consent in which the saved will one day say their amen to everything that he has done and allowed to happen. Laughter is praise of God because it foretells the eternal praise of God at the end of time, when those who must weep here on earth shall laugh.[159]

Part of the rationale for silence is to offer some prospect of times of recollection that not only make prayer possible but also facilitate progress toward wisdom. Blaise Pascal (1623–1662) greatly appreciated the values about which we are reflecting.

> I have discovered that all the unhappiness of men arises from one single fact, that they cannot stay quietly in their own chamber. . . . Hence it comes that men so much love noise and stir; hence it comes that the prison is so horrible a punishment; hence it comes that the pleasure of solitude is a thing incomprehensible. . . . To bid a man to live quietly is to bid him live happily. It is to advise him to be in a state perfectly happy, in which he can think at leisure without finding therein a cause of distress.[160]

In the life of an individual, restraint in conversation often leaves the mind empty of potential distractions not only during the time of prayer but also while engaged in other occupations. Silence facilitates the intense concentration that is of the essence of flow. It also leaves more time available for the serious business of lectio divina and other useful reading. Silence also clears the mind of the stimulants we receive in talking to others.

Silence not only provides the environment for prayer, it progressively becomes the content of prayer. Contemplative prayer is an attentive and respectful stilling of the voice, the imagination, and the mind in anticipation of the Lord's presence, slowly revealed. As prayer develops it tends to become less wordy until, at last, it needs only a few words to frame it. "Few words but many meanings," as Martin Luther described the kind of prayer Jesus recommended in the Sermon on the Mount. Even within this minimalist context a deeper and richer wordlessness can emerge. Sometimes, "there is silence in heaven for half an hour" (Rev. 8:1). Monastic tradition insists that this is a relatively rare experience, especially in the beginning. More often than not the silence experienced in prayer is the simple act of waiting for the body and mind to become still so that God's voice may be more clearly heard. Then we keep watch for the Lord's coming. We pray not with many words, as Saint Benedict says (RB 52.4), but with tears of compunction and heartfelt desire.

Loving Father,
You have called us to come apart
And to give ourselves more fully
To seeking you and finding you.
Grant that our daily lives
May be so shaped by this silent search
That as we go forward
We may be transformed from glory to glory
Into a fuller likeness to Christ,
Who lives and reigns with you in the unity of the
   Holy Spirit,
One God for ever and ever.
Amen!

CHAPTER FOURTEEN

The Grace of Community

Forty years ago Nicholas Humphrey, a professor of psychology at the London School of Economics, proposed the idea that the emergence of creative intelligence in human beings correlates with community living.[161] In his study of the evolution of animal behavior he concluded that living in community makes you smarter. This is because essential tasks are shared, there is more leisure, more time to think of creative solutions, the possibility of pooling knowledge and experience, the possibility of collaboration on tasks too great for one, and the incremental growth of knowledge from one generation to the next.

The resultant development of culture in more complex groups allows for the interaction between independent cells and the emergence of "objective culture" with the effect of increasing the quality of "subjective culture" in each—people become more fully human and alive. The possibility of affective community and intimacy supports and energizes.

But all common life involves renunciation. An individual may be born to a group, but continuance in the group is not automatic. Some species encourage individual existence to increase the prospect of survival of the species, but, for most, the benefit of running with the herd means accepting group standards and, in particular, its structures of dominance. This necessarily involves curtailment of some individual possibilities. The individual will must yield to the common will. The advantages of running with the herd are considered greater than the disadvantages in conforming to social expectations and rules.

Living in an intentional community means that participation in community life is, at the outset, chosen not assigned, and membership is built up on the basis of each having a personal goal that corresponds to the finality of the particular group.[162] After a period of mutual examination an individual may choose to join the group. To become a member, applicants have to be prepared to accept a different identity, often ritualized by an initiation ceremony in which the candidate is, as it were, reborn. This transition is signaled by external changes, such as carrying a members' card, wearing a badge, or performing obligatory rituals.

Let us consider the concrete example of a monastic community. I realize that not everyone lives in a monastery, but I think it is preferable for me to speak from my personal experience rather than trying to imagine alternative situations. In any case, I would hope that whatever I say in whatever context would be received into the reader's own fund of experience and there tested for its applicability. Let me add, by way of superfluous comment, that in our post-truth era it is not a bad idea to submit everything we hear or read to the test of our own knowledge and experience. Otherwise we will surely end up confused.

In monasteries, new recruits often receive a new name, adopt a new form of clothing, and sometimes are given a new haircut, such as a tonsure. The recruit is required to abandon components of the lifestyle that was previously followed; nowadays, for example, this may involve relinquishing some of their opportunities for social media. Internally, there are other more fundamental demands: adopting means appropriate to the common goal of the group, cultivating appropriate beliefs and values, having a different attitude to sexuality, having a different attitude to authority, having a different attitude to self-assertion, having a different attitude to others. Underlying all this is the challenge of being open to the mystery of an invisible world, where the rules and expectations current in ambient society are not always relevant.

Monastic community obviously demands a good deal of renunciation—not as some sort of additional quality, but of its very nature. All who join a monastery give up something precious, not least of all their future. Renunciation continues throughout monastic life. Furthermore, renunciation not only is external, but also progressively becomes both more internal and more radical as progress is made. Renunciation applies also in liturgy. The consolation received from liturgical participation may progressively become rarer and less intense, paving the way for the inrush not only of frivolous distractions but also with sundry irritations about the liturgy itself. To remain in prayer becomes something of a struggle. And in the act of contemplation renunciation reaches its culmination insofar as it involves stepping apart from all that is accessible through sense or intellect. And at the end is the call to eternal life: ultimate renunciation. The point made by Gregory the Great, however, is important to remember: detachment is possible only by a parallel attachment. People are prepared to give up something only when they have taken hold of something better. First the treasure is discovered in the field, and only then is everything sold to enable the purchase of the field and its treasure.

In the third of John Cassian's *Conferences*, attributed to Abba Paphnutius, there is mention of a triple renunciation.[163] The first stage is that the recruit must leave family, home, wealth, career, and make the transition to become a monk. The second is a matter of changing our way of life, struggling against our vices—both bodily and spiritual—and growing in purity of heart. This takes most of a lifetime, and it involves the process of living as a monk, following an authentic monastic life. Then, beyond this is the transfer to eternity (even in this life), when the weight of the monk's attention is spontaneously drawn away from everyday happenings to permit a more intense movement at the level of spirit. The contemplative life progressively involves being seduced from the world of sense into the spiritual sphere. There is a "passion for the unseen" and the consequent dissociation from what is not of God. This is ultimate renunciation, and it leads to radical self-transcendence.

Systematic lack of renunciation is a major cause of malaise in the monastic life, as elsewhere. We soon become aware of this by observing (of course, with a charitable eye) those who are unhappy. Whether this is cause or effect, often the same people exhibit a lack of fervor in their daily life, perhaps without even trying to maintain a decent level of observance. Their state is signaled by narcissistic attitudes, tepidity, behavior inconsistent with their commitments, a chronic tendency to conflict, acedia, generalized lack of enthusiasm for common projects, situational depression, alienation, and eventual departure. A grim reality, but not one that we can afford not to notice.

The principal demand of monastic life is the reasonable renunciation of self-will, and this is true of any lifestyle that brings people together. This brings us back to the important distinction between the outer self and the deep self. Authentic spiritual life involves living from the heart, from the deep self: this means renouncing the primacy of self-will. This is not suppression but ordering: the ordering of love: *ordinatio caritatis*, loving more that which has higher intrinsic worth. You might remember a text I quoted earlier from Thomas Merton on the false self: "All sin starts from the assumption that my false self, the self that exists only in my egocentric desires, is the fundamental reality of life to which everything else in the universe is ordered." The false self is best observed when it is crossed. When it gets what it wants it is like a cat that has swallowed the cream; but if its least whims are thwarted, there will be spitefulness, tantrums, and sulky withdrawals at least and, maybe, some form of active or passive aggression.

We really need to build up our appreciation that self-will or individualism is a major force in subverting the quality of any community. After examining the demise of so many of the intentional communities that sprang up in the 1960s and 1970s, Matthew Ridley concludes thus: "Again and again in accounts of these communities, what brings them down is not the disapproval of the surrounding society . . . but the internal tension caused by individualism." Religiously inclined communities with a reference point outside themselves had a better survival rate, but all alike were crippled and many were destroyed by the impossibility of eliminating rampant individualism.[164]

The building of *affective* communion depends on having first established a functional community that has operated for some time and has been successful, not only in achieving some of the goals set forth in its manifesto but also in creating an everyday harmony and a sense of satisfaction among the members. It should be pointed out that the definition of functional community is gender-specific. Things are done differently in communities of men and in communities of women. In mixed communities the dynamics are even more complex. Creating an *effective* community requires acceptance of common goals, objectives, and means. This means that one who joins the community must sacrifice nonconcordant goals, objectives, and means. Happy perseverance depends on the continuance of the same disposition beyond the phase of initial enthusiasm. In particular, this requires the subordination of "self-will" to the "common will."[165] This renunciation lays the groundwork for a fully contemplative life. Renunciation of self-will means freedom from its tyranny; that is to say, it is openness to self-transcendence. In other words, the flowering of the "deep self" necessarily requires the taming of the "superficial self." On the other hand, individualism brings about the death of community.

Individualism seems to be a universal human tendency, but it is always an obstacle on the way to full human maturity and a cause of retardation in spiritual growth. It seems that sometimes its cause is psychological pathology, since the root of the antisocial behavior is deep and hidden. In monasteries and other institutions that have a period of initial probation, it does not always manifest itself during the early years, but only in the relative "freedom" that comes with acceptance or final profession. To win the attention desired, the behavior becomes more and more bizarre. Eventually it becomes a way of life, rationalized but not really understood.

In such cases where extreme individualism is pathological is there a possibility of a change or a cure? Helping such a person means uncovering the hidden reason for the behavior. This is work for a professional therapist—someone who stands outside the local situation and is skilled in counseling. Inevitably, exploring such issues will generate anxiety, resentment, and anger, and directing these feelings in a creative way requires expertise. It is not a job for amateurs!

Individualism is more than mere eccentricity, showing off, attention-seeking, or odd behavior. According to Pope John Paul II in *Veritatis splendor*, individualism involves an implicit rejection of the social element in human nature.[166] It refuses to others any right to provide input on how I live my life. This is what the medieval monks termed *singularitas*. We have already quoted this text from Baldwin of Forde, but it is worth seeing again. "If someone lives only for himself and for his own advantage, and considers only himself in deciding how he should live, we can understand [this whole life] to be wholly dark."[167]

The medieval monks believed that the fundamental delusion in singularity is that while thinking we belong to ourselves, we allow ourselves to be taken over by the devil. In modern terms this means although we believe ourselves to be autonomous and to be acting spontaneously, the reality is that we are motivated by unconscious drives. Like a virus in a computer, subpersonal tendencies influence our choices without making themselves known. In making ourselves the ultimate determinant of action, a law unto ourselves, we separate ourselves from God and from love, and we precipitate ourselves into a state where sin is inevitable. Even without overt rebellion we have alienated ourselves from God's will and from any prospect of progress in prayer. The relationship with God is impaired if not completely ruptured, and other relationships suffer as the result of this. As our contact with God is weakened, self-destructive behavior increases. Maybe it will be only at the end of our life that we will begin to appreciate that searching for happiness and pleasure apart from God leads only to misery.

The result of chronic self-will is a delusional sense of autonomy; we enter into the belief that we are submitting to no outside authority. Such a state blinds itself to the rights, desires, and sufferings of others. Although it may seek to establish a relationship of domination over others by imposing its rule on them, isolation and alienation will inevitably follow. Seeking to be subtly superior to others, individualists continually assert themselves at the expense of the common life and the common expectations and conventions and, not surprisingly, find themselves somewhat excluded from the common affection. Singularity is a disorder: it sets aside the order willed by God because it fails to prioritize what is truly important and, instead, acts according to its own scale of values. It is a sin against communion, and it becomes a source of division and disharmony in the community.

Because Western culture is individualistic and other cultures are fast becoming so, most of us have been formed in this way. It is noticeable even in monasteries that, because of insecurity, newcomers may try to carve out a niche for themselves, so as to have something distinctive to claim as their own. If this continues and is widespread, it becomes difficult for a community to maintain harmony among so many different "needs" and demands. Sometimes the community surrenders and actively avoids any situation that would demand conversion of its members. Amenities are multiplied so that the inconvenience of sharing is avoided.

The opposite of individualism is mutuality: living in the context of others. When individualism yields to mutuality, selfishness is replaced by sensitivity, conflict is replaced by harmony, stalemate is replaced by dialogue, obstinacy is replaced by adaptability, aggression is replaced by patience, withdrawal is replaced by participation, dysphoria is replaced by euphoria. Of course, this beautiful state is not achieved effortlessly; it demands a lot of self-denial on the part of all.

Building a sense of community that is able to assure stability during the inevitable difficulties that arise is a challenge not only to religious communities but also to business enterprises, which often face a nominal turnover of staff every seven years. One of those who have investigated this phenomenon is Benjamin Chaminade, who arrived at the idea of the centrality of mutual trust in securing continuity and retention. He termed this process of building up a shared loyalty *fidélisation*.

> *Fidélisation* is the voluntary action by which a business establishes an environment that maintains the attachment of the employee over a long period. This enduring and constant attachment which binds the employee to the business is based on shared values. . . . Putting in place a policy of *fidélisation* consists in placing persons and their expectations at the heart of the business concerns so that the professional satisfaction of the employee is assured and a relationship of mutual confidence is established.[168]

Chaminade understood the principal barriers to *fidélisation* to be these: inept management, poor training, lack of recognition or rewards, no communication about the future, and, above all, lack of listening. "If your talented people are not happy you have to find out why."

Listening requires some degree of compassion: a respectful understanding of what another is experiencing. Trying to hear what others are observing, feeling, or requesting, and communicating back what we have heard by body language and by the use of paraphrase. Above all listening and compassion require an acceptance of, a respect for, and even a welcoming of those things that make others different.

Here are some other texts in which Saint Bernard shows himself both aware of the challenges posed by community living and the necessity for each of us to work hard on our relationships with others in the community. Note that this requires no dramatic effort but merely an everyday attention to politeness, courtesy, and respect for others. And a good degree of tolerance until such time as perfection is achieved.

> You will live sociably if you have a zeal to be loved and to love; to show yourself as pleasant and accessible, to support not only patiently but gladly, the weaknesses of your brothers, their weaknesses both of behavior and of body.[169]

In other words, our first obligation in community life is to make ourselves lovable. We do this by being available and treating people well and not being unduly disturbed by their infirmities or their misconduct. If we live like this people will probably love us, and, then, there is a good chance that it will not be too difficult to love them back.

> Because you are placed in a community you are to give precedence to the things that others want over the things that you want. In this way, you will remain among the brothers not only without quarrels but also pleasantly, bearing all and praying for all.[170]

In other words, to avoid quarrels and to be able to be pleasant to all we have to be prepared to put up with their occasional idiocies, to pray for them (especially if they are hostile), and, above all, not to be always pushing our own preferences. We must learn to give way in things that do not matter so that when we insist on something everyone will know that the issue is important to us.

Then your love will be both temperate and just if something is withdrawn from your own pleasures and made available for the needs of a brother. In this way fleshly love also becomes social, since it is drawn out into what is common.[171]

In other words, love becomes more spiritual as it becomes less selfish and it becomes less selfish by giving to others what may legitimately be considered as belonging to oneself. This may be a matter of lending without expecting repayment. It may also consist in letting another take sole credit for a success in which they played only a minor part, or allowing another to claim an authority that is more rightfully one's own.

There are three things which make a person a saint: sober living, upright behavior and a right attitude. He lives soberly if his life is continent, sociable and obedient, that is, if he lives chastely, lovingly, and humbly. Chastity is acquired through the practice of continence. Love is acquired through the practice of sociability and humility through obedience.[172]

In other words, the practice of ordinary sociability will lead us to love. We do not begin the journey to perfect charity by an effusive affection inflicted on all comers. We begin with civility, courtesy, politeness, respect. In ordinary circumstances, we do not seek to overwhelm the other by our disproportionate love, but to allow mutual affection to grow step by step, as it were, naturally. To make ourselves noticeably more loving than the other is to elevate ourselves into a position of superiority and, thereby, to belittle the other person.

> Love is maintained and increased by a friendly expression,
> a pleasant word, a cheerful deed.[173]

In other words, keep smiling. This is not exactly high mystical teaching, but it surely makes sense. I seem to remember Pope Francis making reference to "sourpuss" expressions as being neither reflective of gospel living nor conducive to the spread of the Good News.

Despite what was said in the last chapter about silence, friendly conversation is one of the six means of monastic formation listed by the thirteenth-century Cistercian Adam of Perseigne.[174] Certainly, Saint Teresa of Ávila seems to have been in no doubt about the importance of recreation in community.[175] Adult encounter is not the same as the idle chatter rejected by so many monastic legislators. It is a means of consolidation of relationship, not merely the passing of time or the communication of information. This conversation implies a mutual presence or hospitality, the giving of time and space to another. To play around with the famous saying of Marshal McLuhan, we might say the conversational medium is not only the message, it is also the massage; it eases the pains of social interaction. Of course, massage is not the same as friction, which is likely caused by chronic noncommunication. The main obstacles to fruitful conversation are lack of leisure, overwork, lack of patience, excessive search for entertainment, competitiveness, ambition, and long-lasting animosities.

Saint Benedict gives a certain emphasis to what he terms "mutual obedience" as being the way by which progress is made toward God (RB 71.1–2). Institutional obedience looks after itself; it is enshrined within the context of implicit rewards and punishments. On the other hand, mutual obedience, letting others have their way, is gratuitous. As it happens, the theme was not much developed by Saint Benedict himself nor in subsequent tradition, apart maybe from some remarks by Saint Aelred and quite a serious treatment by Abbot de Rancé of La Trappe (1626–1700). Mutual obedience is not management theory, is not consensus-seeking, is not empowerment of the individual, is not the overthrow of authority. It is, in fact, the extension of the scope of obedience and an increase in its ascetical content, and it certainly brings about the death of self-will.

Medieval Cistercian monasteries saw themselves as schools of charity and love. The basis of fraternal relationships in the monastery is the fact of a shared life, *koinos bios*. This community of experience and of goal, the acceptance of a common tradition and discipline, creates a fundamental harmony between brothers or sisters that is able to minimize the inevitable difficulties of living together. Another factor is also required. Love flourishes to the extent that instinctual behavior is controlled. The greatest obstacles to the growth of love in any relationship are those aspects of life that are ruled by the instincts, that are not subject to the guidance of free, personal decision. Monastic life, because it aims at a degree of freedom from instinctual domination (*apatheia* or purity of heart), creates a climate in which love flourishes naturally and without distortion. The affective life necessary for building strong community is not so much a sentimental attachment as the disciplined, mature, and noninstinctual desire for the other's good. It is an "ordered" love, as distinct from the disordinate movements of the passions. This is not to say that it lacks affective warmth and is cool, conceptual, and controlled. It means rather that there is question of *agape* before *eros*, the welfare of the other before self-gratification—be it patent or disguised.

The best indicator of a community that is both effective and affective is that it encourages all its members (and not just a few) to keep growing, to use their gifts, to develop new talents, and finally, to reach the point of fulfillment intended by God in creating them. In this way the community shows itself to be generative: deploying all the resources of its members in handing on a life-giving tradition to future generations.

The question of recognizing and utilizing the full range of our gifts is one that should concern everyone, especially those who are seeking to live an authentic spiritual life. As Parker Palmer wrote, "The deepest vocational question is not 'What ought I to do with my life?' It is the more elemental and demanding 'Who am I? What is my nature?'"[176] Recognizing one's real nature with its limits and potential is part of the task of self-knowledge. God grants each community, monastic or otherwise, many different gifts, spread among many different persons. The shared life will be vibrant and vital to the extent that all are encouraged to discover, own, make use of, and develop their particular giftedness in the service of the community, the Church, and the world. Gifts will never be uncovered in a group where work or other activities occupy the whole of available time. Leisure is required. The discovery and development of gifts is an essential part of the functioning of any pastoral or leadership position.

The emergence of a generative culture is possible only where the demon of envy is banished. It is as though there are not enough opportunities for growth to go around, so I must seize what is available before it is given to someone else. And then I must cling to it with all my might. It is the conviction that the only way I can enrich myself is to impoverish someone else. Saint Aelred regarded envy as the diametric opposite of charity. "Nothing so provides a feast for the devil as envy, nothing so delights or refreshes him." He continues at some length before concluding:

> Be on your guard, my dearest sons, beware of this disease
> which takes a man wholly away from himself, from his
> neighbor, and from God and makes him wholly subject
> to the devil. Believe me, my brothers, there is nothing that
> so diminishes the joys of this present life or removes the
> hope of future happiness or simultaneously undermines all
> the other virtues [as envy]. How can the envious mind be
> rekindled by the sweetness of charity or enlightened by the
> light of knowledge since there is nothing in it but bitterness
> and darkness?[177]

When people are envious it is usually because they do not see the whole picture. Every gift has its obligation. Every talent cries out to be employed. Every light casts a shadow. Effortless performance is achieved only at the cost of years of laborious practice. The envious person often neglects the downside of brilliance, exalting the one who is the object of their envy into some kind of superior being who is immune from human struggle and toil. But behind this false perception lurks a large measure of self-hatred. Envy suspends both the perception and the employment of one's own particular giftedness. Instead of saying, "You may well play Rachmaninoff like an angel, but I can cook a superior soufflé," one frets at the other's stellar performance and downgrades and despises one's own. The loathing directed at the other is really a twisted substitute for one's own attitude toward oneself. By negating appropriate self-love, envy destroys the capacity for welcoming, accepting, and loving others.

A modern commentator from outside the Christian tradition is equally negative about envy, particularly because of the damage it does to the one who allows it entry.

> Whatever else it is, envy is above all a great waste of mental
> energy. While it cannot be proved whether or not envy

is part of human nature, what can be proven, I believe, is
that, unleashed, envy tends to diminish all in whom it takes
possession. Wherever envy comes into play, judgment is
coarsened and cheapened. However the mind works, envy,
we know, is one of its excesses, and as such it must be identified and fought against by the only means at our disposal:
self-honesty, self-analysis and balanced judgment.[178]

The opposite of envy is a sense of solidarity in which I take
delight in the use and expansion of the talents of others and see my
own as of value insofar as they can be of such benefit to others that
my gifts may be seen as not only mine but also theirs. Baldwin of
Forde was insistent on this point.

[Charity] loves to have things in common, not to possess
them individually without sharing them. . . . Individual gifts
are led by [charity] to [serve] the common good, and a gift
which one person has received as his own personal possession becomes of benefit to another because its usefulness is
shared with him. . . . Someone who has should share with
those who have not, as we are taught by him who says,
"give, and it shall be given to you." . . . Whoever has the
utterance of wisdom or knowledge, whoever has the gift of
work or service, whoever has any other gift, whether greater
or lesser, should possess it as having been given by God for
the sake of others. He should always be afraid that a gift he
has received may turn against him if he does not strive to
use it for the benefit of others, for we receive the gift of God
in vain if we do not use it to seek the glory of God and the
benefit of our neighbor. But if the personal gift which some
[have received] from God is turned to the common good,
it is then that this gift is changed into the glory of God, and
when the gift given to each one individually is possessed in

common through the sharing of love, then the fellowship of the Holy Spirit is truly with us.[179]

Here a word of caution may be helpful. Sometimes it is easier to feel compassion and to give time and attention to those who are struggling and who seem weak and not very gifted than to offer encouragement and support to the talented—a kind of preferential option for the poor. This may leave those with considerable talents out in the cold. This kind of exclusion is a subtext in Ayn Rand's novel *Atlas Shrugged*. The weak make *us* feel needed. When we help them we feel better in ourselves and, so, we cherish the opportunities to do good to them. In a sense, we are exploiting them in order to achieve some mild level of self-satisfaction. The danger is that we may leave them in their weakness because it feels good to us. In addition, they may not wish to overcome their disability because our attention is a kind of reward for not being strong. This is what Martin Seligman termed "learned helplessness." On the other hand, we may envy and resent the strong. We may not understand the gifted. We may think that the talented can care for themselves. We may forget that future quality depends on present creativity. Gifts given to one belong to all, and so it is for the common good that genuine giftedness be encouraged, wherever it occurs. We need to remember that, generally, the more gifted the person, the more help may be needed to integrate giftedness and humanity—to say nothing of spiritual living. In addition, it is probably true that where there is great brilliance there are also deep shadows, even when they are not obvious.

Community living poses many challenges, but it is also the source of many blessings. In a sense, each little Christian group is a mini-Church, responsive to the call of Christ and responsible to him. His summons to live in love is attractive and speaks to our heart, but it is neither simple nor easy to put into practice for years and decades. That is why communities called to live together can accomplish this mission only on the basis of a deep communion with the Lord in whose name they gather.

Lord Jesus Christ,

You have promised that where two or three gather in your name

You are in their midst.

Help us to live together in harmony and peace

So that all who see us may say

"See how they love one another."

For you are our Lord, for ever and ever. Amen!

CHAPTER FIFTEEN

The Grace of Communion

I n this final chapter I plan to speak about the role of solidarity in our spiritual journey. We do not and cannot travel alone. In the first place our journey is a participation in the return of Jesus to his Father—there is an intra-Trinitarian aspect in the spiritual life. We are members of the "whole Christ," and it is only through Christ and in the power of the Holy Spirit that we go to God. As members of Christ's body, we are joined with all the other members, in a special way with Mary the Mother of Jesus and the Mother of the Church, and with all the saints.

We get an inkling of this if we enter the Cathedral of Our Lady of the Angels in Los Angeles. The almost infinite variety that constitutes the assembly of the saints is well illustrated in the tapestries created by John Nava to adorn the side walls. To walk down the central aisle toward the altar is to join a procession of 136 holy people, drawn from every nation, race, tribe, and language. One glance at the walls confirms the belief that there is no such thing as a stereotypical saint. Saints come in all shapes and sizes; men, women, children, ascetics, and people who enjoy life, simple folk and those who are brainy, the powerful and the dispossessed. As participants in the communion of saints we all share a single journey, we are all traveling to eternity, and we travel together.

Our journey is also strongly influenced by our own network of contacts—both the immediate community in which we live and move and have our being, and the extended community with which our relationships are more sporadic. We do not travel alone. The quality of our total experience of the journey to God can be upgraded by taking small steps to improve any or all of these different components.

We need to learn to approach the Church in a mystical, sacramental, theological way, not just sociologically. It is easy for us to be influenced by media reports about "the Church," that have in view merely the earthly institution transacting with secular society. There is no denying that this visible component is real, but the Church is more than that.[180] And it is more than a group of people that come together on Sundays for various worthy reasons and take up a group identity. "The confusion of community romanticism with the communion of saints is extremely dangerous. The communion of saints must always be recognized as something established by God. . . . It is thus willed by God before all human will for community."[181] We do not have to construct the Church: the faithful are brought together to form the Church by the call of God.

The spiritual journey is not such that it can be accomplished alone. We cannot go to God without the helps provided to us by the Church, which is the ongoing presence or memory (*anamnesis*) or sacrament of Christ in the world. Through the proclamation of the word and the celebration of the sacraments it continues Christ's ministry of salvation, leading all to the knowledge of the truth and teaching them to share in the more abundant life offered to members of his body.

By its continual proclamation of the kingdom of God, its insistence on gospel values, and its support in living in the light of these realities, the Church prevents our attempts at pursuing a Christian life from becoming vague, abstract, and subjective. To follow Christ means taking our lead from him, and this is only possible by close adherence to the living reality of the Scriptures, embedded as they are in the life of the Church. Surely it is our own experience that, if we were left entirely to ourselves, our spiritual fervor would quickly wane and our principles of living would become more and more eccentric. Human beings are social animals and so are designed to receive from others whatever is beyond their capacity to provide for themselves. This is true in many practical areas, but it is also true of our spirituality. We receive from other believers nourishment for our souls, guidance for our behavior, encouragement in our weakness, and, sometimes, correction when we slip away from our ideals. However theologians may grapple with its precise meaning, the axiom "outside the church is no salvation" (*extra ecclesia nulla salus*) could very well be interpreted as meaning that we are unlikely to complete the spiritual journey alone; we need other people. Those who are gifted with salvation receive the gift together.

It is through its sacramental life that the Church adds visibility to the work that God is doing in us. Our personal act of faith and our entry into fellowship with other believers is not just an interior act. It is made visible in symbolic form by our accepting baptism. We cannot baptize ourselves, just as we cannot absolve ourselves from sins committed. This requires the instrumentality of the Church. We are sustained on our journey by the frequent celebration and reception of the Eucharist, our *viaticum*, our bread for the journey. This is to fulfill Christ's command to perpetuate his memory through the visible and symbolic act of participating in the Eucharistic meal. In all the sacraments, the Church endows the different aspects of our life with blessing, helping us through visible, tangible, and social forms to perceive the active presence of Christ and his Holy Spirit bringing us to holiness.

The development of a personal ecclesial sense is a credible indication of spiritual progress. My life is not just about myself, trying to achieve salvation, trying to upgrade my living so as to serve others better. My life is mystical participation in the life of Christ, a reality that is not mine alone, but is shared with all who are "in Christ." This is the point at which the spiritual life aims. Its early stages, however, are usually more individual, but that changes with time and progress.

In the beginning, the conversion to a more intense spiritual life is usually marked by a strongly affective devotion to the person of Jesus. This is the fuel that energizes whatever steps we take to make our discipleship an effective part of daily life. It is to be expected that, as the years pass and we make some progress, the form this devotion takes will adapt itself to the changing circumstances of our life—both inner and outer. It can happen that somewhere along the line we lose the sense of a personal relationship with Jesus and our spirituality becomes rather too abstract. In that case, we have to renegotiate the relationship.

Bernard of Clairvaux chronicles this evolution in his treatise *On the God Who Must Be Loved* (*De diligendo Deo*). Our love for God needs to pass from the self-centered to the more ecstatic; real love in its perfection draws us away from ourselves, makes us self-forgetful, totally engaged with the God of infinite lovableness. Our progression through the different stages—if we may so call them—of love may be compared to an education of our spiritual palate. Slowly we are drawn away from the grosser and more sugary pleasures of the beginning toward subtler and—may we say—more sophisticated delights: from the "flesh" to the "spirit." As love becomes purer it displaces the more carnal tendencies of our nature, which, otherwise, would have a dominant influence over the choices that we make.

Our attitude to the humanity of Jesus has to move away from sentimental images that appeal to us at an emotional level to a zone that is deeper, more spiritual, and, ultimately, more energizing. This is to say our attention drifts from the earthly career of Jesus as recounted in the Gospels to his risen life, present in our midst. Bernard quotes the text of 2 Corinthians 5:16 eighteen times, and even when it is not explicitly cited it lurks behind many of the passages that embody his Christology. "If we have known Christ Jesus according to the flesh, we know him thus no longer." Another favorite text was "Christ the Lord is a spirit before our face" (Lam. 4:20), which he quotes twenty times. The mystery of Christ's life that is at the center of his spirituality is the Ascension. He understands this in a particular way. He sees the Resurrection not as a mere return to life (*reditus*)—as was the case with Lazarus, the daughter of Jairus, and the young man of Nain—but as a *transitus*, a matter of passing into a different mode of being. This was witnessed by the spirituality of Jesus's body in the post-Resurrection appearances, appearing and disappearing, passing through walls. The Ascension marks a complementary transition from an existence that is anchored to specific points in the spatiotemporal continuum to an existence that is atemporal or, more properly, omnitemporal. Jesus is now—by virtue of the mystery of the Ascension—present at all points in space and in time. St. Leo said as much in his second sermon for the Ascension: "Just as the Lord did not depart from the Father when he descended, so he did not depart from his disciples when he ascended."[182] But Bernard goes further than this. Christ is now *more* present to us in mystery than he ever was in history. Perhaps the most important preposition in the New Testament is "with." Christ is our Immanuel: "Behold I am with you all days until the consummation of the age" (Matt. 28:20).

The only possible response to Christ, our God with us, is one of love. The love about which Bernard speaks is not adolescent hero worship or sentimental attachment to a product of our imagination. It is a spiritual love—one generated in us by the Holy Spirit who has been given to us. To say that it is spiritual in cause, however, is not to affirm that it is abstract or unfeeling. We are, after all, commanded to love with our whole heart, with our whole soul, and with all our strength. For Saint Bernard this means that our love for Christ is to be comparable to Christ's love for us. Just as he is for us "a dear friend, a wise counsellor, and a strong helper," so our love for him must be warm, rational, and strong.

> O Christian, learn from Christ how you are to love Christ. Learn to love sweetly, to love prudently, and to love strongly. Sweetly, so that we are not seduced [by pleasures]; prudently, so that we are not deceived [by errors]; strongly, so that we are not turned away from love of the Lord by oppression. So that you are not led astray by the world's glory or by the pleasures of the flesh, let Christ's wisdom be a greater source of sweetness than they are. So that you are not seduced by a spirit of falsehood and error, let Christ's truth become your light. So that you are not wearied by adversities, let Christ the power of God be your strength. Let charity influence your zeal, let knowledge give it direction, and constancy be its strength. Let your zeal be fervent and careful and unconquered. Let it not be lukewarm or lacking in discernment or fearful.[183]

Our love for Christ must be characterized by an affective intensity (*zelum affectionis*). It must be governed by reason so that it is vigilant and cautious, wary of the possibility of going astray, of "being zealous without knowledge," according to the phrase of Romans 10:2, a citation Bernard uses eighteen times. Our love needs to be strong, vigorous, and, he would say, "manly," able to overcome the difficulties and obstacles that beset its path. This is a love that has a good measure of robustness, able to withstand failure and disappointment. It should be fairly clear from this that, as far as Bernard was concerned, love for Christ was not merely a feeling of devotion in times of fervent prayer but a guiding principle throughout life. An experiential love for Christ that goes beyond a vague sense of being united with him motivates us to be attentive to his teaching and to imitate his attitudes and actions—and to retain our composure in those inevitable passages of life when we are called to participate in his Passion.

As we have already noted, our adult devotion to Christ progressively leads us to see our spiritual lives as belonging not only to us but as being an expression of the life of Christ's body—what was called in the era of Pope Pius XII the "mystical body of Christ," the Church. We are of the Church, and whatever transpires in our lives is of relevance to the whole of God's people. This is made astonishingly clear in the creative and untranslatable vocabulary of Ephesians 3:6: one inheritance, one body, one sharing. This solidarity becomes clearer in the latter stages of prayer's development when we become more and more conscious that what comes forth from the depths of our Spirit is not only our own voice; it is the voice of the Church. Our most intimate prayer is simultaneously the prayer of all God's faithful people. This is, of course, especially true when we celebrate the liturgy, but it is also true of all prayer. We are members of Christ's body; we are not alone. We live and pray with all the saints; we look forward to sharing eternity with them. We belong to the household of God; the saints are our fellow citizens. We can, as one of the Prefaces in the Missal reminds us, profit from their teaching, their example, and their intercession.

In a preeminent way this applies to our relationship with the Mother of Jesus, proclaimed by Pope Paul VI as "Mother of the Church." Not every Christian has the same conscious awareness of the role of Mary in our spiritual life. Taking for granted that this doctrine is true, we have to suppose that eventually it will make itself known to us. In this as in other matters, we do not all follow an identical chronology; what happens to some early on is late-onset for others. We should, however, be prepared to take tradition seriously and accept the word of those who are experienced in such matters—at least to avoid excluding the possibility.

In 1937 the John Rylands Library in Manchester published a fragment of a Greek papyrus (#470) that had originated in Egypt about the year AD 250. On it was written the earliest-known prayer to Our Lady, here—nearly two centuries before the Council of Ephesus—addressed in the vocative case as *Theotokos*, "The One who gave birth to God" or "Mother of God." The full text of the prayer could be reliably reconstructed since the prayer itself is well attested in later Greek and Coptic liturgical texts, and there are two Latin versions of it—one Roman and one Ambrosian. This ancient prayer is the *Sub tuum praesidium*, "We fly to your protection, O holy Mother of God, despise not our prayers in our necessities, but deliver us from danger, O ever-glorious and blessed Virgin."

This is a clear indication that from about the time of Origen, and especially in the church of Alexandria, during periods of danger and crisis, the Church turned to Mary as a help and protection. The papyrus prayer probably originated during the Decian or Valerian persecutions of the third century, but it continued in use in the Latin, Byzantine, Coptic, and, eventually, Slavonic liturgies in the centuries that followed, even up to the present day. From this we can deduce that Mary has been seen as a source of help and protection for individual Christians and for the Church as a whole for nearly eighteen hundred years. Even if we are Marian minimalists, it is not a bad prayer to have at hand.

There are other holy people who populate our spiritual lives; we will all have our own favorites. The age-old practice of venerating the saints helps us to keep our feet on the ground, to see the grace of God acting in different circumstances and bringing to holiness persons of different talents and temperaments. Their example can inspire us, and, to the extent that we achieve some level of identification with them, their words can serve as a source of guidance on our own journey. Above all, the reality of God's saints—both those universally recognized and those less well-known—is a source of confidence and celebration. We see the grace of God effectively transforming humble humanity into the "noble creatures" we were created to become.

And there are yet other saints who are even closer to us. I mean the family or community in which we live and the people who make up our daily lives. These have all been created with a unique dignity and the capacity to image God, destined to grow in likeness to their divine exemplar. This is especially so when they have been consecrated by baptism and have allowed the grace of this sacrament to permeate their lives. Whatever the twists and turns of their particular journey, we are all traveling together to the same destination. And we are called to help one another, to have a zeal that those around us reach that point of growth intended by God in creating them. When everyone has a zeal for self-actualization the result is a sense of mutual belonging that tends toward deep communion. As Teilhard de Chardin was wont to observe, "What ascends must converge." Any effort we put into building more effective and affective relationships will eventually help to make of us more of a communion than simply a group that lives or does things together or simply collides on the road of life. As I insisted in the last chapter, working on areas of politeness and thoughtfulness, sincere mutual respect, exalting compassion over judgment, committing ourselves to cooperation and mutual service, avoiding ambition, meanness, bossiness, bullying, and the like will eventually make us a more sociable, affable, friendly, and unified group with a capacity for dialogue.

The grace of communion is really an anticipation of heaven, and so it is unlikely to be fully realized here on earth. It remains our goal, the destination of our journey. We do not travel alone, we travel together. We are for one another sources of encouragement, guidance, and practical help. As we approach the end of the road we will find that we are closer together. And for all the toil involved in traveling, we are always the beneficiaries of God's enabling grace that continually invites us to leave our comfort zone and go beyond our limits. This is not a cause for dread or dismay. There is a grace and an energy at work carrying us upward that does not stem from our own limited resources. All we have to do is to learn to get with that strength, to allow it to bear us up and try to restrain the stupidity that makes us want to seize the controls. "It is God who, according to his good purpose, is at work in [us] both to will and to act" (Phil. 2:13). May God bring to completion the good work that he has thus begun unto the day of Christ Jesus. Amen.

Loving Father,
You have called us together
As members of the body of your Son.
May we be zealous to preserve the unity of the Spirit,
Which is the bond of peace,
And so, with all the saints,
Come to know the mystery of Christ's surpassing love
And so be filled with all the fullness which is of God.
We ask this in the name of Jesus, our Lord. Amen!

NOTES

INTRODUCTION

1   Georges Bernanos, *The Diary of a Country Priest* (London: Boriswood, 1937), 371. To his friend's regret that another priest had not arrived to assist him on his deathbed, the "Country Priest" replied, "'Does it matter? Grace is . . . everywhere.' I think he died just then."

2   See Massimo Faggioli, *Sorting Out Catholicism: A Brief History of the New Ecclesial Movements* (Collegeville, MN: Liturgical Press, 2014). "Today, world Catholicism is experiencing a particular historical moment in which the influence of Catholic movements is particularly strong," (x.) Also, Brendan Leahy, *Ecclesial Movements and Communities: Origins, Significance, and Issues* (New York: New City Press, 2011).

1. THE GRACE OF DISCONTINUITY

3   *Lumen gentium*, chapter 5: *De universali vocatione ad sanctitatem in Ecclesia*. In the English translation edited by Austin Flannery this is reduced to "The Call to Holiness," modifying the specific word "vocation" to something more generic, as well as eliminating the note of universality. *Vatican Council II: The Conciliar and Post Conciliar Documents* (Collegeville, MN: Liturgical Press, 1975), 396.

4   The word *become* is often not translated in English versions.

5   Thomas S. Kuhn, *The Structure of Scientific Revolutions*, 4th ed. (Chicago: University of Chicago Press, 2012), 175.

6   Translated from Basil the Great, *On the Holy Spirit* 15.37; SChr 17, 169. Basil's image of a brief pause between the end of the first and the beginning of the second may be optimistic. Sometimes the discontinuity between stages, when the old is dying and the new is yet to be born, endures for a considerable time and, in the intervening void, gives rise to uncreative tendencies that grow stronger the longer the interregnum lasts.

7   It may be noted that there is much in contemporary culture that
    encourages us to be inattentive to the quality of the choices we make and
    encourages us to develop a kind of "learned helplessness." We abandon
    personal responsibility in favor of algorithms and automation on the
    one hand ("automation bias") and on the other to compliance with a
    multitude of self-reproducing bureaucratic regulations. For some years,
    tourists blindly following their GPS used to end up in the farm paddocks
    of our monastery, gazing bewilderedly at the cows and wondering what
    to do next. If they had used their heads and paid attention either to the
    road signs or to their surroundings this would not have happened.

8   As Clive James remarked about himself, autodidacts tend to overrate
    themselves. "Waking up in Europa," *Times Literary Supplement* 5907 (17
    June 2016), 15.

9   Bernard of Clairvaux, QH 12.1; SBOp 4, 457: *Qui enim in circuitu
    ambulat, proficiscitur sed proficit nihil.*

10 Bernard of Clairvaux, SC 9.2; SBOp 1, 43: "By [God's] grace I have now,
    for many years, been careful to live chastely and soberly. I have insisted
    on reading and resisted vices. I have frequently taken on the burden of
    prayer. I have been vigilant against temptations. I have thought over my
    years in the bitterness of my soul (Isa. 38:15). As far as I could I judge
    that I have lived among my brothers without contention. I have been
    submissive to higher powers, going out and coming in at a senior's
    command. I have not desired what belongs to another but in the sweat
    of my brow have I eaten my bread. But as far as concerns all this, it has
    been a matter of routine; there has been no delight" (*Totum constat de
    consuetudine, de dulcedine nihil*).

11 See Bernard Lonergan, *Method in Theology* (London: Darton, Longman
    & Todd, 1971), passim. Note especially the following: "conversion is a
    change of direction and, indeed, a change for the better. One frees
    oneself from the unauthentic. One grows in authenticity. Harmful,
    dangerous, misleading satisfactions are dropped. Fears of discomfort,
    pain, privation have less power to deflect one from one's course.
    Values are apprehended where before they were overlooked. Scales
    of preference shift. Errors, rationalizations, ideologies fall and shatter
    to leave one open to things as they are and to man as he should be"
    (52). And, "By conversion is understood a transformation of the
    subject and his world. Normally it is a prolonged process though its
    explicit acknowledgment may be concentrated in a few momentous
    judgments and decisions. Still it is not just a development or even a
    series of developments. Rather it is a resultant change of course and
    direction. It is as if one's eyes were opened and one's former world

faded and fell away. There emerges something new that fructifies in inter-locking, cumulative sequences of developments on all levels and in all departments of human living" (130).

12   Aelred of Rievaulx, S. 65.14; CCCM 2B, 174: *Vocati sumus exteriori aemulatione, bonorum aemulatione, occulta inspiratione.* See also S. 116.4; CCCM 2C, 176. Abba Paphnutius in John Cassian, *Conferences* 34; SChr 42, 142–43. Also Antony of Egypt, *Letter* 1 translated by Derwas J. Chitty in *The Letters of St Antony the Great* (Oxford, UK: Fairacres, 1975), 1–2. See also Smaragdus of Saint-Mihiel: "The call of the divine kindness, which is made in different ways in different ages and at different times, is not due to human merit but is always made freely by God alone in his kindness. . . . People are called in different ways, as was said. Some who are healthy only in body are called, as are other afflicted with weakness of the flesh are called, as are others again who are oppressed by diverse defects or various trials. They are called at different ages: some in infancy, some in adolescence, others in youth, others in old age; and some even in extreme old age." *The Crown of Monks*, translated by David Barry, osb (Collegeville, MN: Cistercian Publications, 2013), ch. 50; "On the Call of Divine Kindness," 127.

13   John Cassian, *Conferences* 3.4; SChr 42, 142.

14   John Cassian, *Conferences* 9.26; SChr 54, 63.

15   Isaac of Stella, S. 17.16: *Mutata ergo affectio cordis necessario permutat exercitium corporale*: "A change in the affection of the heart necessarily changes bodily behavior."

16   "Now like him I've started sighing for no reason / *Just that time when . . . If only I'd . . .* / All the haunting almosts and the one implacable was." Blake Morrison, "Old Men Sighing," in *Shingle Street* (London: Chatto and Windus, 2015).

17   This was noted by John Cassian in *Institutes* 8.8; SChr 109, 346.

18   For a more positive presentation of the reality of aging see Notker Wolf, *Aging Starts in Your Mind: You're Only As Old as You Feel*, trans. Gerlinde Büchinger-Schmid (Brewster, MA: Paraclete Press, 2017), and Joan Chittister, *The Gift of Years: Growing Old Gracefully* (Katonah, NY: BlueBridge, 2010).

19   "Old men who are moderate and not difficult or inhumane experience old age as tolerable; frowardness and inhumanity will be troublesome at every age." *Moderati enim et nec difficiles ned inhumani senes senectutem*

tolerabilem agunt, importunitas et inhumanitas omni aetati molesta est.
Cicero, *De senectute* 37.

20   Bernard of Clairvaux, Div 13.4, SBOp 6a, 133.

21   Bernard of Clairvaux, *De misericordiis* 4; SBOp 6a, 42–43.

22   This is the title of Patrick White's 1981 autobiography.

23   Bernard of Clairvaux, PP 3.7; SBOp 5, 196.

2. THE GRACE OF DESIRE

24   "Thanks to our evolutionary past, we are wired to feel dissatisfied with
our circumstances, whatever they may be. An early human who was
happy with what he had—who spent his days lazing on the savannas of
Africa thinking about how good life is—was far less likely to survive and
reproduce than his neighbor who spent every waking moment trying
to improve his situation." William B. Irvine, *On Desire: Why We Want
What We Want* (New York: Oxford University Press, 2006); 176.

25   "This always working to perfect / That which by nature must remain
imperfect." Geoffrey Hill, *Broken Hierarchies: Poems 1952-2012* (Oxford:
Oxford University Press, 2014).

26   André Ardouin, "Desire for God According to Gregory of Nyssa,"
Tjurunga 17 (1979): 89–108. Daniel O'Donovan, "Gregory of Nyssa's
Epektasis," *Colloquium* 4 (1970): 54–61. Isabelle Bochet, *Saint Augustin
et le désir de Dieu* (Paris: Études Augustiniennes, 1982). Michael Casey,
"Spiritual Desire in the Gospel Homilies of St. Gregory the Great," csq
16 (1981), 297–314. Michael Casey, *Athirst for God: Spiritual Desire in
Bernard of Clairvaux's Sermons on the Song of* Songs (Kalamazoo, MI:
Cistercian Publications, 1988). Lode van Hecke, *Le désir dans l'expérience
religieuse: L'homme réunifié: Relecture de Saint Bernard* (Paris: Cerf,
1990). Michael Casey, "Desire and Desires in Western Tradition,"
Tjurunga 71 (2006): 62–92.

27   Augustine of Hippo, *Expositions on the Psalms* (Corpus Christianorum
Series Latina XXXVII-XL). *128*, 8, 4; CChr 40, 1688.

28   "The qualitative *content* of the numinous experience, to which 'the
mysterious' stands as form, is in one of its aspects the element of
daunting 'awefulness' and 'majesty'. . . but it is clear that it has at the
same time another aspect, in which it shows itself as something uniquely

attractive and *fascinating*." Rudolf Otto, *The Idea of the* Holy, trans. John W. Harvey, 2nd ed. (New York: Oxford University Press, 1980), 31.

29 Friedrich Schleiermacher, *On Religion: Speeches to Its Cultured Despisers*, trans. John Oman (New York: Harper and Row, 1958), 26–101, "The Nature of Religion."

30 See Michael Casey, "*Suspensa Expectatio*: Guerric of Igny on Waiting for God," *Studies in Spirituality* 9 (1999): 78–92.

31 "The truly 'mysterious' object is beyond our apprehension and comprehension, not only because our knowledge has certain irremovable limits, but because in it we come upon something inherently 'wholly other,' whose kind and character are incommensurable with our own, and before which we therefore recoil in a wonder that strikes us chill and numb." Otto, *Idea of the Holy*, 28.

32 Theologically speaking—as distinct from experientially—the term *musterion* in the New Testament refers to the saving action of God that takes place outside the sphere of human rationality or causality—as evidenced in the resurrection of Jesus. The believer's contact with the *musterion* is explained as being taken up into the "mystery of Christ," of being relocated within the divine economy of human salvation in a way that eludes rational analysis. This is a theological interpretation of an experience that, even after the explanation, remains nebulous and forever full of mystery.

33 See Casey, "Desire and Desires," 62–92.

34 The term was developed on the basis of Song 2:4: *ordinavit in me caritatem*. On this see the seminal article by Maur Standaert, "Le principe de l'ordination dans la théologie de S. Bernard," *COCR* 8 (1946): 176–216.

35 Thomas Merton, *The Climate of Monastic Prayer*, CS 1: (Spencer, MA: Cistercian Publications, 1970), 121.

36 Resu 4.2; SBOp 5, 111.

37 Cassian, *Conference* 1; SChr 42, 77–108.

3. THE GRACE OF HUMANITY

38 Robert Javelet, *Image et ressemblance au douzième siècle: De saint Anselme à Alain de Lille* (Paris: Éditions Letouzey & Ané, 1967), 1:x.

39 Larry Siedentop, *Inventing the Individual: The Origins of Western Liberalism* (London: Penguin, 2015).

40 See Eva Carlotta Rava, *Caída del hombre y retorno a la verdad en los primeros tratados de San Bernardo de Claraval* (Buenos Aires: EDUCA, 1986).

41 *Interior House* 80; PL 184, col. 547CD

42 SC 27.10; SBOp 1, 188–89.

43 Paul Tillich, *The Courage to Be* (London: Collins, 1967), 90. The "self" to which Tillich refers was qualified in an earlier part of the paragraph (89–90). "The affirmation of self as self, that is of a separated, self-centred, individualized, incomparable, free self-determining self . . . separation is not estrangement, self-centredness is not selfishness, self-determination is not sinfulness. They are structural descriptions and the condition of both love and hate, condemnation and salvation."

44 See Richard Egenter, *The Desecration of Christ,* trans. Edward Quinn (London: Burns & Oates, 1967): "The saints appear to be raised above the ugly realities of this world and the struggle with sin and the consequences of sin. . . . Kitsch pictures and statues of saints, however, invariably show them in a sort of Christian Arcadia, and to judge from these it would appear that becoming a saint is a gentle, pleasant, but rather boring process. All this is bound to dull the perception of those who regularly pray before such statues" (98–99).

45 In Scholastic terminology, *agere* follows *esse.*

46 Parker Palmer, *Let Your Life Speak: Listening for the Voice of Vocation* (San Francisco: Jossey-Bass, 2000), 49.

47 *Ep. 368*—To Stefano di Corrado Maconi: *Se sarete quello che dovete essere, metterete fuoco in tutta Italia, non tanto costì.*

48 Thomas Merton, *The New Man* (London: Burns & Oates, 1962), 30.

49 Genesis 32:30; in the Vulgate Latin version this was rendered, *Vidi Deum facie ad faciem, et salva facta est anima mea.*

4. THE GRACE OF ALTERNATION

50   See Casey, *Athirst for God*, 251–79.

51   *Gaudium et Spes*, 9, modified.

52   *De Consensu Evangelistarum* 4.10, 20; PL 34, 1227–28.

53   Alfred North Whitehead, *Religion in the Making* (Cambridge: Cambridge University Press, 1927), 6.

54   Bernard of Clairvaux, SC 6.9; SBOp 1, 30.

55   Bernard of Clairvaux, SC 21.10; SBOp 1, 128.

56   See Juana Raasch, "The Monastic Concept of Purity of Heart and Its Sources," *Studia Monastica* 8 (1966): 7–34, 183–214; 10 (1968): 7–56; 11 (1969): 269–314; 12 (1970): 7–43. See also Harriet A. Luckman and Linda Kulzer, eds., *Purity of Heart in Early Ascetic and Monastic Literature: Essays in Honor of Juana Raasch o.s.b.* (Collegeville, MN: Liturgical Press, 1999).

57   Bernard of Clairvaux SC 17.2; SBOp 1, 99.

58   Bernard of Clairvaux SC 21.4; SBOp 1, 124.

59   Bernard of Clairvaux, SC 36.6; SBOp 2, 8.

60   See Michael Casey, "The Virtue of Patience in Western Monastic Tradition," *CSQ* 21 (1986): 3–23. Reprinted in *The Undivided Heart: The Western Monastic Approach to Contemplation* (Petersham, UK: St Bede's Publications, 1994), 95–120.

61   See Michael Casey, "The Value of Stability," *CSQ* 31 (1996): 287–301. Reprinted in *An Unexciting Life: Reflections on Benedictine Spirituality* (Petersham, UK: St Bede's Publications, 2005), 235–57.

62   Stephen Flynn, "America the Resilient," *Foreign Affairs* 87.2 (March/April 2008): 2–8.

63   Bernard of Clairvaux, *Ep.* 136; SBOp 7, 332.

5. THE GRACE OF TEMPTATION

64 Aelred of Rievaulx, S. 54.1; CCCM 2B, 66.

65 Aelred of Rievaulx, *De Oneribus* 24.27; CCCM 2D, 222–223.

66 Saint Augustine, *On Psalm 60*, 3; CChr 39, 766.

67 Jesus's description of food as external to the body is repeated in modern anatomy, which regards the gastric lumen as merely a channel through the body by which food eaten completes its journey. Because the walls are permeable, nutrients can be extracted from the food and thence absorbed into the body.

68 W. B. Yeats, "The Circus Animals' Desertion," in *Collected* Poems (London: Macmillan, 1978), 392.

69 Evagrius of Pontus, *Praktikos* 6; SChr 171, 508.

70 Aelred of Rievaulx, S. 56.18; CCCM 2B, 96.

71 Mary Oliver, "Hum, Hum," in *A Thousand Mornings: Poems* (New York: Penguin, 2012), 42–43.

72 "More than half a century ago, while I was still a child, I recall hearing a number of older people offer the following explanation for the great disasters that had befallen Russia: Men have forgotten God; that's why all this has happened. Since then I have spent well-nigh fifty years working on the history of our Revolution; in the process I have read hundreds of books, collected hundreds of personal testimonies, and have already contributed eight volumes of my own toward the effort of clearing away the rubble left by that upheaval. But if I were asked today to formulate as concisely as possible the main cause of the ruinous Revolution that swallowed up some sixty million of our people, I could not put it more accurately than to repeat: Men have forgotten God; that's why all this has happened. . . . The failings of human consciousness, deprived of its divine dimension, have been a determining factor in all the major crimes of this century." Sourced from roca.org.

73 S. Giora Shoham, *Society and the Absurd* (Oxford: Blackwell, 1974), 1–26: "Accidia and the Absurd: A Conceptual Discussion."

74 I have covered this topic in *Strangers to the City: Reflections on the Beliefs and Values of the Rule of Saint Benedict* (Brewster, MA: Paraclete Press, 2005), 39–44.

75   Neil Postman, *Amusing Ourselves to Death: Public Discourse in the Age of Show Business* (New York: Penguin, 2005). This is a re-edition of a book first published in 1985.

76   *Appetitus vanitatis est contemptus veritatis; et contemptus veritatis est causa nostrae caecitatis.* Bernard of Clairvaux Ep 18.1; SBOp 7, 67.

77   I am reminded of what Theodore Roszak wrote half a century ago: "The greatest single victory bourgeois society has won over even its most irreconcilable opponents is the fact that it has inculcated in them its own shallow reductionist image of man." *The Making of the Counter-Culture* (London: Faber & Faber, 1970), 100.

78   Aelred of Rievaulx, S. 72.26; CCCM 2B, 239.

79   Bernard of Clairvaux, QH 2.1–2; SBOp 4, 389–390.

80   Dorotheos of Gaza, *Discourses* 1.8; SChr 92, 158.

81   Translated from Julian of Norwich, *Revelation 14*, chapter 61; in Edmund Colledge and James Walsh, ed., *A Book of Showings to the Anchoress Julian of Norwich* (Toronto: Pontifical Institute of Medieval Studies, 1978), 2, 603.

82   Translated from Julian of Norwich, *Revelation 14*, chapter 48; 2, 501–502.

83   Joachim Jeremias, *New Testament Theology: Volume One* (London: S.C.M. Press, 1971), 147–48.

84   What follows is a riff on a paragraph in Aelred's S. 54.18; CCCM 2B, 73: "As I have said, the first thing is that we must detest this vice under which we perceive ourselves to labour. Then, as often as its delight takes hold of us, let us accuse ourselves liberally so that sometimes we receive bodily necessities with tears and never without grief. After this let us carefully make a case against this vice and listen to others who point it out and rebuke it. Finally, and this is the most necessary thing of all, let us ask [God] with whom all things are possible that this vice may be extinguished. [Let us do this] with many prayers and deep sighs, with great contrition of heart and tears. And let us judge those to be happy who have escaped the slavery of the body and ourselves as wretched since we are weighed down by this weakness."

85   Aelred of Rievaulx, *Homeliae de oneribus propheticis Isaiae* 26.6; CCCM 2D, 235.

6. THE GRACE OF SELF-KNOWLEDGE

86 As recounted by Kevin Rudd, then Australian Prime Minister, on *Late Night Live* (November 6, 2012); www.abc.net.au/rn. See also Jean Baudrillard, "Postmodernity is said to be a culture of fragmentary sensations, eclectic nostalgia, disposable simulacra, and promiscuous superficiality, in which the traditionally valued qualities of depth, coherence, meaning, originality, and authenticity are evacuated or dissolved amid the random swirl of empty signals." Available at www. azquotes.com/author/1049-Jean_Baudrillard.

87 Thomas Merton, *Faith and Violence* (Notre Dame, IN: University of Notre Dame Press, 1968), 112.

88 Quoted in John Eudes Bamberger, *Thomas Merton: Prophet of Renewal* (Kalamazoo, MI: Cistercian Publications, 2005), 77.

89 "The Inner Experience: Notes on Contemplation (I)," CSQ 18.1 (1983), 3.

90 Thomas Merton, "The Inner Experience (I)," CSQ 18.1 (1983), 9.

91 Merton, *The New Man*, 30.

92 Thomas Merton, *New Seeds of Contemplation* (London: Burns & Oates, 1962), 27–28.

93 Thomas Merton, *Love and Living* (New York: Farrer Strauss Giroux, 1979), 196, 199.

94 Baldwin of Forde, *Spiritual Tractate VI*, in *Spiritual Tractates, Volume One: Tractates I-VIII*, trans. David Bell (Kalamazoo, MI: Cistercian Publications, 1986), 169.

95 Aelred of Rievaulx, S. 43.5; CCCM 2A, 337.

96 "Now in all societies there is a limit to which *society* (institutions) can help the individual in any formal way when alienation at the private level of identity occurs." Barry Shenker, *Intentional Communities: Ideology and Alienation in Communal Societies* (London: Routledge & Kegan Paul, 1986), 33.

97 Bernard of Clairvaux, Resu 3.3; SBOp 5, 505.

98 Bernard of Clairvaux, Resu 3.4; SBOp 5, 106–7.

99   Bernard of Clairvaux, SC 36.5; SBOp 2, 7.

100 Aelred of Rievaulx, S. 3.21; CCCM 2A, 31.

101 It was well described by Lucretius in *De rerum natura*. "It is pleasant when, on the great sea the winds disturb the calm, / to watch from land the great labor of another; / not that it is a source of joy or pleasure that another is in trouble / but it is pleasant to see that of such evils you yourself are free." Lucretius, *De rerum natura* 3.1–4; J. H. Warbuton Lee, ed., *T. Lucreti Cari: De Rerum Natura Libri I-III* (London: Macmillan, 1950), 39. *Suave, mari magno turbantibus aequora ventis, / e terra magnum alterius spectare laborem; / non qui vexari quemquam sit iucunda voluptas, / sed quibus ipse malis careas quia cernere suave est.*

102 "Swink & sweat in all that thou canst & mayest for to get thee a true knowing & a feeling of thyself, a wretch, as thou art. & then I trowe that soon after that thou shalt have a true knowing & a feeling of God as he is . . . as he voucheth safe to be known & feeled of a meek soul living in this mortal body." *The Cloud of Unknowing* 14.42.

103 SC 83.1; SBOp 2, 298–99.

7. THE GRACE OF PRAYER: PETITION

104 Saint Augustine, *On the Psalms* 29.2, 1; CChr 38, 174.

105 Aelred of Rievaux, *De institutione inclusarum* 28; CCCM 1, 661–62.

106 Rudolf Bultmann, *The Gospel of John*, trans. G. R. Beasley-Murray (Oxford: Basil Blackwell, 1971). The section on pp. 203–84 is titled "The Revelation as *krisis*."

107 Maurice Nédoncelle, *The Nature and Use of Prayer*, trans. A. Manson (London: Burns & Oates, 1964).

108 *Conferences* 9.8; SChr 54, 48–49.

109 *Self-Reliance* 2.79 3: "men's prayers are a disease of the will."

8. THE GRACE OF PRAYER: DEDICATION

110 Eugene Boylan, *Difficulties in Mental Prayer* (Dublin: Gill and Macmillan, 1943). New edition from Ave Maria Press, Notre Dame, IN, 2010.

212 | GRACE *On the Journey to God*

111 Flannery O'Connor, *The Habit of Being*, ed. Sally Fitzgerald (New York: Farrar, Straus, Giroux, 1979).

112 "& perforce take good keep into tyme, how that thou dispendist it. For nothing is more precious than tyme." *The Cloud of Unknowing* 4.20.

113 Nédoncelle, *The Nature and Use of Prayer*, 12.

114 Saint John Climacus, *The Ladder of Divine Ascent*, trans. M. Heppell (London: Faber, 1959); Step 28, #34; 255.

115 Some older readers might remember *The Hippopotamus Song* from the English comedic duo Flanders and Swann: "Mud, mud, glorious mud. / Nothing quite like it for cooling the blood. / So follow me, follow, / down to the hollow / And there let us wallow in glorious mud."

116 Quoted in Ian Ker, *John Henry Newman: A Biography* (Oxford: Oxford University Press, 1988), 94.

9. THE GRACE OF PRAYER: CONTEMPLATION

117 Note the following quotation, remembering that at this stage in his book the author is examining prayer from human to human as a basis for understanding prayer to God. "If we except the border-line case of an administrative request, prayer is contemplative, and it is this, as we have just noted, that distinguishes it from a declaration. It needs a personal presence. . . . The contemplation involved in prayer is, therefore, active; it is bound to cause some change in you or in me. . . . Prayer is a form of contemplation which usually has to deal with the obstacle of distance; even so, it is never uttered in a night so dark that the person to whom it is addressed is completely inaccessible." Nédoncelle, *Prayer*, 8–9.

118 This chapter includes some passages from *Towards God: The Western Tradition of Contemplation*, rev. ed. (Blackburn: Dove, 1995), 160–71.

119 *The Book of Privy Counsel*, [chapter 6]; 152.

120 See Michael Casey, "*Intentio Cordis* (RB 52:4)," *Regulae Benedicti Studia* 6/7 (1977/1978): 105–21. Reprinted in *An Unexciting Life*, 335–58.

121 Merton, *Climate of Monastic Prayer* 121. See also my article, "Thomas Merton's Notes on 'Inner Experience' Twenty-Five Years Afterwards," *Tjurunga* 44 (1993): 30–55. Reprinted in *The Undivided Heart*, 189–217.

122 *Bot trauayle besily in that nouwt. The Cloud of Unknowing* 68.122.

123 Translated from *Revelations*, 14.41; 464–65.

10. THE GRACE OF FAITH

124 Karl Rahner, "Anonymous Christians," in *Theological Investigations Volume Six: Concerning Vatican Council II*, trans. Karl-H. and Boniface Kruger (London: Darton, Longman & Todd, 1974), 390-98. This article is a version of a radio talk originally given in 1964.

125 *Fides instructionem desiderat.* S. 272; PL 38, 1246B.

11. THE GRACE OF REVELATION

126 "From the creation of the world God's unseen qualities—eternal power and divinity—have been clearly seen, being understood from what has been made, so that they are without excuse. For although they knew God, they neither glorified him as God nor gave thanks, but they became empty in their thinking and their unintelligent hearts were darkened. Claiming to be wise, they became fools. They exchanged the glory of the incorruptible God for the images made in the likeness of corruptible human beings, birds, animals, and reptiles. Therefore, God gave them over in the sinful lusts of their hearts to impurity for the degrading of their bodies with one another. They exchanged the truth of God for falsehood, and worshiped and adored the creature rather than the Creator—who is to be blessed for ever. Amen. Therefore, God gave them over to dishonorable passions. . . . Furthermore, since they gave no importance to acquiring the knowledge of God, God gave them over to a depraved mind, to do what ought not to be done. They have become filled with every kind of wickedness. . . . Although they know that in the righteous judgment of God those who do such things deserve death, they not only do these things but they also approve of those who practice them" (Rom. 1:20–32).

127 For a good treatment of the different aspects of the experience of beauty see Patrick T. McCormick, *God's Beauty: A Call to Justice* (Collegeville, MN: Liturgical Press, 2012).

128 *Letter to Marcellinus* 12; trans. Robert C. Gregg, in *Athanasius: The Life of Antony and the Letter to Marcellinus* (New York: Paulist Press, 1980), 111.

129 Karl Rahner, *Hearers of the Word*, trans. Michael Richards (New York: Herder and Herder, 1969).

130 For a fuller treatment of the four senses of Scripture, see Michael Casey, "Levels of Meaning," in M. Casey, *The Art of Sacred Reading* (Blackburn: Dove, 1995), 48–73.

131 Bernard of Clairvaux, Adv 5.2; SBOp 4, 189.

132 Bernard of Clairvaux, Adv 3.2; SBOp 4, 176.

12. THE GRACE OF LEISURE

133 This chapter returns to a number of themes already discussed in *Strangers to the City*, 26–37.

134 See Jean Leclercq, *Otia Monastica: Études sur le vocabulaire de la contemplation au moyen âge* (Rome: Herder, 1963).

135 Mihaly Csikszentmihalyi, *Flow: The Psychology of Optimal Experience* (New York: Harper and Row, 1990).

136 The freedom of which we speak in this section is, to employ the terminology of Jacques Maritain, not so much freedom from obligation as freedom from coercion. Human life, because of its social component, is never free of obligations; we can, however, hope to attain a measure of freedom from coercion, so that we do what we do voluntarily, not because we are compelled by a threat of physical or moral violence.

137 For a detailed sociological study of all aspects of monastic work see Isabelle Jonveaux, *Le monastère au travail: Le royaume de Dieu au défi de l'économie* (Paris: Bayard, 2011).

138 Josef Pieper, *Leisure the Basis of Culture* (New York: Pantheon, 1952), 52.

139 Pope John Paul II, on the contrary, always seemed to be more interested in someone else, looking beyond the person to whom he was speaking and checking out the next person in line. In my own case I have photographic evidence of this.

140 Don De Lillo, quoted in David Remnick, "Exile on Main Street: Don De Lillo's Undisclosed Underworld," *The New Yorker*, September 15, 1997, 43 and 47.

141 Thomas Merton, *The Asian Journal of Thomas Merton* (New York: New Directions, 1973), 117.

142 Max Picard, *The World of Silence* (Wichita, KS: Eighth Day Press, 2002), 8–19.

143 "Have the courage to go against the tide of this culture of efficiency, this culture of waste." Pope Francis, "Homily at XXVIII World Youth Day: 27 July 2013," *L'Osservatore Romano*, 29–30 July 2013, 4.

144 Thomas Merton, "The Inner Experience: Problems of the Contemplative Life (VII)," *CSQ* 19 (1984), 279–80.

145 See Hugo Rahner, *Man at Play: or Did You Ever Practise Eutrapelia?* (London: Burns & Oates, 1965).

13. THE GRACE OF SILENCE

146 Forerunners to this chapter include Michael Casey, "Silence," in *The New SCM Dictionary of Christian Spirituality*, ed. Philip Sheldrake (London: SCM Press, 2005), 582–83. Also a small pamphlet: *Listening to God: The Value of Silence in the Spiritual Life* (St. Meinrad, IN: The Abbey Press, 2010).

147 Alfred North Whitehead, *Religion in the Making* (Cambridge: University Press, 1927), 6.

148 Susan Cain, Quiet: *The Power of Introverts in a World that Can't Keep Quiet* (New York: Crown/Archetype, 2013).

149 Bernard of Clairvaux, Div 17.2; SBOp 6a, 151: *dissoluta, impudica, magniloqua, dolosa, maledica.*

150 Bernard of Clairvaux, Div 27.5; SBOp 6a, 201: *scurrilitates, detractiones, iactantiae et impatientiae verba.*

151 Bernard of Clairvaux, Div 55.1; SBOp 6a, 280: *Verbum stultum, vanum, mendax, otiosum, dolosum, maledicum, impudicum, excusatorium.* Isaac of Stella's examples of inappropriate speech include "vain words, lies, contentious or destructive words, detraction, boasting, covetous or sexual words and any coarseness." S. 38.9; SChr 207, 310.

152 Bernard of Clairvaux, Hum 28–30, SBOp 3, 38–40.

153 Bernard of Clairvaux, Div 17.5; SBOp 6a, 154.

154 Bernard of Clairvaux, *Quad* 3.4. SBOp 4, 367.

155 See Michael Casey, "Restraint of Speech," in *A Guide to Living in the Truth: Saint Benedict's Teaching on Humility* (Liguori, MO: Liguori/ Triumph, 2001), 159–78.

156 Richard Sennett, *Together: The Rituals, Pleasures and Politics of Cooperation* (New Haven: Yale University Press, 2005). "The social engine is oiled when people do not behave too emphatically. The subjunctive mood is most at home in the dialogical domain, that world of talk which makes an open space, where discussion can take an unforeseen direction. . . . By practising indirection, speaking to one another in the subjunctive mood, we can experience a certain kind of sociable pleasure: being with other people, focusing on and learning about them, without forcing ourselves into the mould of being like them" (23).

157 Gerard Loughlin, reviewing Rowan Williams's book *On Christian Theology*, in *Times Literary Supplement*, 4 August 2000.

158 Aelred of Rievaulx, S. 158.14; CCCM 2C, 478–79. But note also S. 103.8 (CCCM 2C, 94), where Aelred remarks, "We do not read that Jesus ever laughed."

159 Karl Rahner, *The Great Church Year: The Best of Karl Rahner's Homilies, Sermons, and Meditations* (New York: Crossroad, 1993); quoted in Mary Stommes, ed., *Give us This Day: Daily Prayer for Today's Catholic: September 2012* (Collegeville, MN: Liturgical Press, 2012), 137. Similarly, in an article on Jewish humor, Jeremy Dauber writes: "The kind of laughter that the Bible *does* prize is that of those who are in sync with the divine plan for the world, and who are on the right side of God's covenant." From "It's a Funny Old Testament," *The Tablet* 271, no.9227 (November 25, 2017): 8.

160 Blaise Pascal, *Pensées* 2.139; trans. W. F. Trotter, in *Great Books of the Western World* (Chicago: Encyclopaedia Britannica, 1990), 30, 196–197.

14. THE GRACE OF COMMUNITY

161 Nicholas Humphrey, "The Social Function of Intellect," in *Growing Points in Ethology*, ed. P. G. Bateson and R. A. Hinde (Cambridge: Cambridge University Press, 1976), 303–317. Available at www. cogprints.org/2694/1/socialfunctiontext.pdf

162 "An intentional community is a relatively small group of people who have created a whole way of life for the attainment of a certain set of goals." Shenker, *Intentional Communities*, 10.

163 John Cassian, *Conferences* 3.6.1; SChr 42, 145. English translation by Boniface Ramsay in *John Cassian: The Conferences* (New York: Newman Press, 1997), 123. "Now something must be said about the renunciations which the tradition of the fathers and the authority of Holy Scripture show to be three and which each one of us ought to pursue with all our zeal. The first is that by which in bodily fashion we despise all the wealth and resources of the world. The second is that by which we reject the erstwhile behaviour, vices and affections of soul and body. The third is that by which we call our mind away from everything that is present and visible and contemplate only what is to come and desire those things that are invisible." This text is similar to a text of Evagrius of Pontus in *On Thoughts* (*Peri logismon*) 26; SChr 438, 172.

164 Matt Ridley, *Nature via Nurture: Genes, Experience and What Makes Us Human* (London: Fourth Estate, 2003), 230.

165 On this concept see Michael Casey, "Merton's Teaching on the 'Common Will' and What the Journals Tell Us," in *The Merton Annual: Studies in Culture, Spirituality and Social Concerns* 12 (1999): 62–84. There is an important qualification to be made. It is incorrect to identify the "common will" with the whim of a superior. It is the superior's task to allow the common will to become visible, not to replace it with his or her own preferences.

166 John Paul II, *Veritatis Splendor* 32: "There is a tendency to grant to the individual conscience the prerogative of independently determining the criteria of good and evil and then acting accordingly. Such an outlook is quite congenial to an individualist ethic, wherein each individual is faced with his own truth, different from the truth of others. Taken to its extreme consequences, this individualism leads to a denial of the very idea of human nature."

167 Baldwin of Forde, *Spiritual Tractate VI*, 169.

168 Benjamin Chaminade, "Fidélisation versus retention," 8 June 2003, translated from www.focusrh.com/article.php3?id_article=107.

169 Bernard of Clairvaux, PP 1.4; SBOp 5, 190.

170 Bernard of Clairvaux, Nat 3.6; SBOp 4, 216.

171 Bernard of Clairvaux, Dil 23; SBOp 3, 139. In the treatise *On the God Who Must Be Loved*, Bernard tracks the emergence of purely spiritual love from its earliest stages. The engine that drives the development is the progressive selflessness of the affective tendency. What begins as a simple turning aside from the ways of the flesh proceeds to the highest stages of contemplation and from there it is just a small step into heaven. On this see Michael Casey, "In Pursuit of Ecstasy: Reflections on Bernard of Clairvaux's *De Diligendo Deo*," *Monastic Studies* 16 (1985): 139–56.

172 Bernard of Clairvaux, Div 64.2; SBOp 6a, 297.

173 Bernard of Clairvaux, Div 121; SBOp 6a, 399.

174 Adam of Perseigne, Ep. 5:55; SChr 66, 118.

175 Father Terrence Kardong is of the same mind. See his article "Monastic Recreation," *Tjurunga* 74 (2008): 73–80.

176 Palmer, *Let Your Life Speak*, 15. See also 16: "Our deepest calling is to grow into our own selfhood, whether or not it conforms to some image of who we *ought* to be."

177 Translated from Aelred of Rievaulx, S. 55.6; CCCM 2B, 171.

178 Joseph Epstein, *Envy* (New York: Oxford University Press, 2003), 97.

179 Baldwin of Forde, *Spiritual Tractate XV*, trans. David N. Bell, in *Spiritual Tractates: Volume Two: Tractates IX-XVI* (Kalamazoo, MI: Cistercian Publications, 1986), passim and 185.

15. THE GRACE OF COMMUNION

180 It is surely no surprise that the revelation of widespread sexual abuse and its toleration have caused many of the faithful to become disenchanted with the institutional Church and made them see more clearly the Eurocentrism, patriarchy, insensitivity, incompetence, politicization, and the sheer idiocy of the Roman system of governance. We need to be able to move beyond giving all our attention to the worldwide institution and to concentrate more on living the gospel more comprehensively in a local, communitarian, and personal context. On such matters I found instructive Hans Küng, *Can We Save the Catholic Church? We Can Save the Catholic Church* (London: William Collins, 2013).

181 Dietrich Bonhoeffer, *Sanctorum Communio* (London: Collins, 1963), 195–96.

182 Leo the Great, S. 61.3; SChr 74bis, 280. In the reading from Saint Augustine for the feast there is a similar idea.

183 Bernard of Clairvaux, SC 20.4; SBO p1–2.

ABBREVIATIONS

Adv	Sermons on Advent
CChr	Corpus Christianorum Series Latina (Turnhout: Brepols)
CCCM	Corpus Christianorum Continuatio Mediaevalis (Turnhout: Brepols)
COCR	*Collectanea Ordins Cisterciensium Reformatorum*, later *Collectanea Cisterciensia*
CS	Cistercian Studies Series (Kalamazoo, MI: Cistercian Publications)
CSQ	*Cistercian Studies*, later *Cistercian Studies Quarterly*
Dil	Treatise of Bernard of Clairvaux *On the God Who Must Be Loved*
Div	Miscellaneous or Monastic Sermons in SBOp 6a
Ep.	Epistolae in SBOp 7–8
Hum	Treatise of Bernard of Clairvaux: *On the Steps of Humility and Pride.*
Nat	Sermons on Christmas in SBOp 4
PL	J.-P. Migne, *Patrologia Latina*
PP	Sermons on Saints Peter and Paul in SBOp 5
Quad	Sermons on Bernard of Clairvaux: *On Lent.*
QH	Sermons on Psalm 90 in SBOp 4
RB	Rule of Saint Benedict
Resu	Sermons on Easter in SBOp 5
S.	Sermon
SBOp	*Sancti Bernardi Opera I–VIII* (Rome: Editiones Cistercienses, 1957–1977).
SC	Sermons on the Song of Songs in SBOp 1–2
SChr	Sources Chrétiennes (Paris: Cerf)

Inevitably there is some overlap between this book and others I have written; sometimes a thought is mentioned that is more fully developed elsewhere, and sometimes what I write now has appeared in germ in another book or article. I have written about a dozen books and scores of articles, and it is inevitable that there will be some repetition. Throughout my life, although I keep reading new authors, my principal sources have remained fairly constant. Perhaps it may be clarifying if I list the pillars of my personal approach.

AUGUSTINE OF HIPPO (354–430)

Saint Augustine is one of the most important figures in the development of Latin theology. He was a prolific theological writer and polemicist, but his most influential works have been his more personal and spiritual writings, particularly his *Confessions*, his sermons, and his commentaries on the Psalms and on the Gospel of John, which were much used in the liturgy.

BALDWIN OF FORDE (d. 1190)

Baldwin was born at Exeter and became successively abbot of Forde, bishop of Worcester, and archbishop of Canterbury. He was a well-read scholar, and the *Spiritual Tractates* he composed while abbot are profound personal reflections within the context of monastic tradition. His subsequent career as churchman was ambiguous, to say the least. He took part in Richard I's crusade and died during the siege of Acre.

BENEDICT OF NURSIA (480–547)

Benedict founded the monasteries of Subiaco and Monte Cassino and wrote a Rule that has been the principal authority of Western monasticism. By encouraging his monks to read widely in Christian literature he laid the foundation for the love of learning that is one of the hallmarks of the Benedictine tradition. Although the Rule is a small text, the writings of those who have followed it and have been inspired by it are vast.

BERNARD OF CLAIRVAUX (1090–1153)

Bernard was the principal exponent of the spirituality of reformed monasticism in the twelfth century. The content of his theology was traditional but it was reexpressed in a way that spoke strongly to the experience of his contemporaries. His literary style is warm, fluent, and very persuasive. His interventions in public life were not always well-advised, but it was as a spiritual master that he won a reputation for holiness.

THE CLOUD OF UNKNOWING

The Cloud of Unknowing and *A Book of Privy Counselling* are works by an unknown mystical writer in fourteenth-century England. Written in Middle English, they are characterized by a lyrical style, solid doctrine, and a practical orientation.

EVAGRIUS OF PONTUS (346–399)

Originally from Cappadocia, Evagrius was forced by an indiscretion to take refuge in the Egyptian desert. There he became the theologian of early monasticism, combining the teachings of the Desert Fathers with the speculative framework of Origen. His *Praktikos* (a guide for monks) and his *Chapters on Prayer* and several other works are available in English. Through his influence on John Cassian, his teaching and that of Origen became influential in both East and West.

GREGORY THE GREAT (540–604)

Gregory was a monk who became bishop of Rome. He is the author of many works on the spiritual life including a narrative on the life of Saint Benedict. His spirituality was influenced by both Augustine and Cassian, but his style was easier and more universal than theirs.

ISAAC OF STELLA (1100–1178)

Born in England, Isaac studied in France. Isaac brought to his monastic career a fine mind and a sound education. His works include fifty five discourses and other theological works. His doctrine is profound, strongly influenced by Augustine but with some highly personal positions and an engaging style.

JOHN CASSIAN (360–435)

Cassian was trained as a monk in the deserts of Egypt under the great spiritual masters who lived there. He later founded twin monasteries near Marseille and wrote for their benefit his *Institutes* and his *Conferences* (both available in translation). These works expressed in Latin in a systematic form what he had learned in Egypt, and they were, in particular, a means by which the teachings of Origen and Evagrius reached the West. Cassian influenced Saint Benedict and remained on monastic reading lists for several centuries.

ORIGEN OF ALEXANDRIA (185–254)

Origen was the first major theologian of the spiritual life, interpreting the books of the Bible not only as sources of historical information and doctrine but also as guides to behavior and incentives to prayer. Some of his philosophical and theological ideas were rejected as heretical, but much of his spiritual doctrine became embedded in subsequent mainline tradition.

THOMAS MERTON (1915–1968)

Merton was a Cistercian monk of Gethsemani Abbey in Kentucky and a bestselling author. His range of interests was wide, but he is quoted here for his spiritual doctrine and his teaching on contemplative prayer.

WILLIAM OF SAINT-THIERRY (1085–1148)

William was a significant theologian and Benedictine abbot who was a close friend of Saint Bernard. In 1135, at the age of fifty five he resigned his abbacy and became a Cistercian monk at Signy. He left more than a dozen profound literary works including a *Life* of St. Bernard and the *Golden Epistle*.

ABOUT PARACLETE PRESS

WHO WE ARE

As the publishing arm of the Community of Jesus, Paraclete Press presents a full expression of Christian belief and practice—from Catholic to Evangelical, from Protestant to Orthodox, reflecting the ecumenical charism of the Community and its dedication to sacred music, the fine arts, and the written word. We publish books, recordings, sheet music, and DVDs that nourish the vibrant life of the church and its people.

WHAT WE ARE DOING

Books

PARACLETE PRESS BOOKS show the richness and depth of what it means to be Christian. While Benedictine spirituality is at the heart of who we are and all that we do, our books reflect the Christian experience across many cultures, time periods, and houses of worship.

We have many series, including *Paraclete Essentials*; *Paraclete Fiction*; *Paraclete Giants*; and the new *The Essentials of...*, devoted to Christian classics. Others include *Voices from the Monastery* (men and women monastics writing about living a spiritual life today), *Active Prayer*, the award-winning *Paraclete Poetry*, and new for young readers: *The Pope's Cat*. We also specialize in gift books for children on the occasions of Baptism and First Communion, as well as other important times in a child's life, and books that bring creativity and liveliness to any adult spiritual life.

The MOUNT TABOR BOOKS series focuses on the arts and literature as well as liturgical worship and spirituality; it was created in conjunction with the Mount Tabor Ecumenical Centre for Art and Spirituality in Barga, Italy.

Music

The PARACLETE RECORDINGS label represents the internationally acclaimed choir *Gloriæ Dei Cantores*, the *Gloriæ Dei Cantores Schola*, and the other instrumental artists of the *Arts Empowering Life Foundation*.

Paraclete Press is the exclusive North American distributor for the Gregorian chant recordings from St. Peter's Abbey in Solesmes, France. Paraclete also carries all of the Solesmes chant publications for Mass and the Divine Office, as well as their academic research publications.

In addition, PARACLETE PRESS SHEET MUSIC publishes the work of today's finest composers of sacred choral music, annually reviewing over 1,000 works and releasing between 40 and 60 works for both choir and organ.

Video

Our DVDs offer spiritual help, healing, and biblical guidance for a broad range of life issues including grief and loss, marriage, forgiveness, facing death, understanding suicide, bullying, addictions, Alzheimer's, and Christian formation.

Learn more about us at our website:
www.paracletepress.com or
phone us toll-free at 1.800.451.5006

SCAN
TO
READ
MORE

You may also be interested in...

Strangers to the City
Reflections on the Beliefs and Values of the Rule of Saint Benedict
Michael Casey

$15.99 Trade paper
ISBN 978-1-61261-397-0

"Casey knows what Benedict is trying to say. And he knows how to apply it to the modern world."
—Terrence Kardong, OSB, author of *Benedict's Rule: A Translation and Commentary*

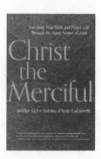

Christ the Merciful
Victor-Antoine d'Avila-Latourrette

$16.99 Trade paper
ISBN 978-1-61261-772-5

"This is rich spiritual fare, the wisdom of millennia seasoned with one monk's profound personal experience of prayer and suffering." —Mike Aquilina, author of *Angels of God: The Bible, the Church and the Heavenly Hosts*

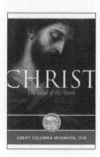

Christ
The Ideal of the Monk
Columba Marmion, OSB

$16.99 Trade paper
ISBN 978-1-612-61573-8

This book, an abridged edition of the original, examines the writings of St. Paul and St. John in the light of the Gospels and offers spiritual understanding to any Christian's religious life.

Available through most booksellers or through Paraclete Press:
www.paracletepress.com | 1-800-451-5006
Try your local bookstore first.